PRODUCTIVITY SAND TRAPS & TAR PITS

PRODUCTIVITY SAND TRAPS & TAR PITS

HOW TO DETECT AND AVOID THEM

MIKE WALSH

Dorset House Publishing
353 West 12th Street
New York, New York 10014

Library of Congress Cataloging-in-Publication Data

Walsh, Mike. 1937–
    Productivity sand traps and tar pits / by Mike Walsh.
       p. cm.
    Includes bibliographical references and index.
    ISBN 0-932633-21-8
    1. Industrial productivity. 2. Management information systems.
3. Software productivity.   I. Title.   II. Title: Productivity sand traps
and tar pits.
    T58.8.W35   1991
    658.4'038--dc20   91-21441
                                                      CIP

Cover design by Jeff Faville, Faville Graphics. Chapter opening graphics from *Handbook of Pictorial Symbols* with permission from Dover Publications, Inc. (Copyright © 1976 by Dover Publications, Inc.). Quotations on pages 71, 135, 185 from *Barnes & Noble Book of Quotations* (New York: Barnes & Noble, 1987). Material in chapters 2, 12, and 13 evolved from *Realizing the Potential of Computer-Based Information Systems* by Myles E. Walsh (New York: Macmillan Publishing Co., 1984).

dBase III Plus® is a registered trademark of Ashton-Tate. TOTAL is a product of CINCOM. IDMS® is a registered trademark of CULLINET. VTAM is a trademark, CICS® and IBM® are registered trademarks, and IMS/VS and OS/MVS are products of International Business Machines Corporation. Lotus® and 1-2-3® are registered trademarks of Lotus Development Corporation. Metaphor® is a registered trademark of Metaphor Computer Systems. Oracle® is a registered trademark of Oracle Corporation. PICK® is a registered trademark of PICK Systems.

Copyright © 1991 by Dorset House Publishing Co., Inc., 353 West 12th Street, New York, NY 10014.

Distributed in the English language in the United Kingdom, Ireland, Europe, and Africa by John Wiley & Sons Ltd., Chichester, Sussex, England. Distributed in the English language in Japan and Southeast Asia by Toppan Company.

Printed in the United States of America   12 11 10 9 8 7 6 5 4 3 2 1
Library of Congress Catalog Card Number 91-21441
ISBN: 0-932633-21-8

For
Richard Walsh

Acknowledgments

Voltaire once said that originality is nothing but judicious imitation. If they are honest, authors must recognize that much of their thought is more derivative than original. All of us learn what we know from those with whom we've been associated. In all that we do, we must acknowledge the contributions made by others.

Professionally, I've spent thirty-six of my fifty-four years working in the information systems field, where I have developed and implemented systems, managed projects, served as instructor and consultant, and written articles and several books. On a personal level, I have learned much from being a husband and a father of four sons, and from independently studying sociology, psychology, law, religion, economics, and philosophy.

As a result of my experience, I have reached only one conclusion about personal and professional life that I consider close to absolute: None of my conclusions are absolute. Since life is a mixture of successes and setbacks, of changes in perspective, my conclusions are in a constant state of adjustment. However, I have collected in this book those conclusions about productivity that I have found perpetually true.

In accordance with Voltaire, I acknowledge that I am a collector of lessons learned by myself and others. I am a purveyor of commonsense truths. My conclusions about how to work productively were formulated as I read books, as I worked with other people, and as I attended classes and seminars. It was in a university classroom that I was introduced to the work of the pioneers of productivity improvement, people like Frederick Taylor and Frank and Lillian Gilbreath. Later, I learned from the more contemporary work of Douglas McGregor, Tom Peters, Tim Lister, and Tom DeMarco.

There is, of course, no way to mention all of the people who have influenced my work, but some deserve credit here. First, I thank my wife, Diana, who keeps me honest. Janice Wormington and Wendy Eakin, at Dorset House, worked patiently for over a year to get me to articulate in an orderly way the lessons of my experience. David McClintock, my editor, went over the manuscript completely. Some authors complain about editors messing with their manuscripts; David made nothing but improvements. Although we struggled a bit from time to time, I am grateful for his contribution. All of us need to be accountable to someone; we writers need our editors to filter what we produce before revealing it to our readers.

In my twenty-three years at CBS, I learned how to be productive within an intensely political climate. I learned it from watching others. I thank them for their example, especially Bob Chandler, Dave Allen, Max Pinkerton, Rich Silverman, Mia Mather, Ray Vail, Barbara Opello, John Lalli, Peter Schementi, Michael McSweeney, Frank O'Neill, John Giumarra, Al Kaufman, Dan Johansson, and Roz Blanch.

I am grateful for the help Ted Czochanski gave in the development of the chapter on interpersonal communication. My thanks are extended to Doug Hoyt and Bill Thomson for reading the manuscript for content. While encouraging me, they also offered needed constructive criticism.

Contents

PRODUCTIVITY SAND TRAPS & TAR PITS

Introduction

For many years now, we Americans have applied labels to decades. We had the Swinging Sixties and the Soaring Seventies. The Eighties were labeled by some as the ME decade. I have already seen one proposal that the Nineties be called the WE decade, a notion based on cooperation and teamwork. Judging from recent articles I've read and from personal contact I've had, many people, young and old, are giving guarded support for this proposal.

Historically, Americans have always had a "can do" attitude. It seemed that there wasn't anything that we couldn't do if we just put our minds to it. We were able to produce quality goods and services more effectively and more efficiently than anyone. If someone were to have asked why, we might have responded that we believed in the future and were building for tomorrow. Then, somewhere along the way, we got lost.

Currently, the United States is no longer the best, not even second best—maybe not even in the top ten—in terms of productivity. What happened? Well, there are many Monday morning quarterbacks and armchair generals who will expound at length on what happened. The more important question concerns what we can do to restore our lost productivity. The answer is simple: Improved productivity means getting back to basics.

This book advocates productivity, what Webster defines as "effectiveness in utilizing labor and equipment." This is a top-down dynamic: Only when the people in the trenches believe that their managers are committed to the idea, and that the fruits of increased productivity will be shared with them, can it work. Managers must have respect for the people who actually provide the services or build the products and get them out the door. It takes both effective management and effective production work to get things done.

In order to constantly improve the quality of the goods and services we produce, we need to concentrate on fine-tuning our productivity. Some drastic measures have already been taken to do that. For example, many corporations got too fat, and some of the fat had to be trimmed. This was painful. I can attest to that, since I was one of those who lost a job. However, further improvements in productivity are still possible.

My approach assumes that the obvious inhibitors to improved productivity have been or soon will be eliminated. Instead, I highlight the not-so-obvious sand traps and tar pits that sap productivity in hidden and subtle ways within the information systems field. I propose ways to minimize their impact, such as initiating better methods or procedures, applying technology more judiciously, and improving communication. These basic productivity enhancements are extremely difficult to quantify, but they should not be ruled out, even if they don't appear to be cost-effective in the short term.

Productivity must be measured by effectiveness. The goods and services produced must attain some level of quality. When products and services are inadequate, those producing them are ineffective, no matter how efficient in terms of dollars they may appear. The United States has allowed the quality of its goods and services to slip too far. We lost ground in everything from automobiles to television sets. Information systems seems to be an area in which we have a tenuous lead; but if we're not careful, we may blow that too.

If we can change our orientation to the creation of quality goods and services, abandoning the lust for power and wealth measured in dollars, I believe we can take some significant steps in generating a real wealth in which many can participate. If I am correct in suggesting that an individual's insecurity and anxiety flow from a basic knowledge that his or her productivity is low or nonexistent, then it will certainly pay to find ways to increase the productivity of individuals. Perhaps there won't be as many big winners, but there will be many more smaller winners.

There are four parts to this book. Each is devoted to a different area of the information systems field in which productivity can be improved. Part One identifies two mind-sets that impair management's use of technology and describes ways to apply technology in a more effective manner. Part Two concerns the effective management of human resources, and suggests how management can foster a productive working environment. Part Three consists of five case studies in which productivity successes and failures are shown in real-life contexts. Part Four provides two proven tools toward improving productivity: wisdom (a list of principles, countered by a Machiavellian viewpoint) and work (a simple method of coordinated organizational planning). These four parts direct attention to the subtle factors that obstruct daily productivity—even those impediments that go against basic common sense in their occurrence. While most corporations know how to trim the branches, long-term health depends on tending the disease that attacks the roots.

What I offer are some suggestions that have the potential to bring about small productivity improvements. I believe that we miss opportunities to improve productivity because of oversights. From this comes the title of the book. We have blundered into numerous productivity sand traps and tar pits, such as overreliance on high tech, overspecialization (relying on experts), and breakdowns in communication. We've gotten ourselves into this mess and we're going to have to get ourselves out. I believe that if enough of the suggestions put forth in this book are applied, over time, productivity will improve.

PART ONE
Effective Use of Technology

In these opening chapters, I discuss a number of ways in which productivity is lost through the misuse of information systems technology and computer technology. I stress these two technologies because they, more than any others, permeate every area of our professional and personal lives. The loss of productivity comes about not because the technology is complex, but because many of us are reluctant to publicly acknowledge what we don't understand. As a result, we grant acceptance to plans and products simply because they have been made to appear impressive.

I have seen senior executives remain silent, even as terms and topics they could not possibly have understood would arise, simply because they wanted to appear technologically current. I call this the high-tech syndrome. Productivity loss also occurs when individuals resist change, simply because the initiative comes from another individual or group. They put their own interests ahead of those of the organization. This is what is known as the not-invented-here (NIH) syndrome. The productivity lost through these two syndromes is a slow but steady leak, like that in an automobile's cooling system, which when neglected for too long, leads to a more serious problem. Chapter One examines these two syndromes.

In addition to the loss caused by the high-tech and NIH syndromes, productivity suffers when the technology that we have in place is not fully utilized. Fast changing technology is overwhelming and information systems managers are bombarded constantly by vendors and the trade press with new technology products. Often these products, as remarkable as they might be, represent solutions looking for problems. Technology should provide information systems with the means to fulfill their purpose: to develop and operate systems that service the operational components; to provide meaningful, timely, and accurate information to the executives of an organization. Chapter Two explores some ways in which this can be done.

1

Fixing the Leaks

A leak is often viewed as a petty annoyance. Priorities being what they are, a leak is often considered not significant enough, or not worthy of the time and resources needed to fix it. Consequently, the leak is ignored; but it doesn't stop and only gets worse.

I believe that our country's productivity is suffering due to a multitude of ignored leaks. They all started small but, because we in America were "riding high" in the 1980s, they were not fixed. What were leaks have turned from trickles into torrents. This chapter examines two of these productivity leaks: the high-tech syndrome and the not-invented-here syndrome. Each syndrome is illustrated by four scenarios that show day-to-day contexts, and depict the leakage of productivity through the misuse of technology.

THE HIGH-TECH SYNDROME

If there is a single field that illustrates how badly the basics have been forgotten, it is the high-tech field of computers and information systems. While most of the productivity gains and losses discussed in this book relate to this field, the situations described and the conclusions reached have a more universal application. We have become so enamored with the hype and the mystique of computers and information systems that we frequently opt for the sizzle instead of the steak.

Projects fall short or fail primarily because too much is expected of the technology. When expectations, unrealistic to begin with, are not met, technology takes the rap. Neglected or forgotten are the basics. Expectations were that technology would dot all the i's and cross all the t's. In reality, technology has its limitations, but it is our behavior that enhances or inhibits productivity. Only by accepting responsibility for the problem can we then do something about it. My purpose in the following scenarios is to exhibit ways in which technology is misapplied.

Shifting the Blame

Large information systems are subject to bugs. In a typical integrated systems environment, when a bug comes up, most of the individuals involved scurry off to their workstations to assure themselves that their component is not the cause of the problem. When the cause of the problem is found, attempts are made to shift the blame else-

11

where. Although the problem eventually gets fixed, much activity goes into avoiding responsibility. The bad feelings and mistrust that are generated mitigate against productivity within the environment.

Much more productive would be an environment in which there is an attitude of collective responsibility. In such an environment, when a problem is discovered, individuals from the affected areas immediately get together, find, and fix the problem. The project leaders explain to their superiors what the error was and what they plan to do to see that it doesn't happen again. Despite the fact that there is often pressure to reveal the name of the individual or individuals who caused the problem, they do not reveal it. Then they work together as a group to determine the cause of the problem and take steps to see that it does not recur. In this type of environment, there is more productivity for less time spent. There are no witch hunts and no resultant bad feelings or mistrust.

A wise manager fosters such an atmosphere of cooperation and trust. In such an environment, the members of the team deal directly with the problem, since they do not want their professional image tarnished by a single unproductive individual. I once knew a couple of managers, one named Dan and the other named Jack, who operated this way. They cultivated a spirit of camaraderie among their subordinates. Their teams were loyal and committed. When problems occurred, Dan and Jack took the heat. The names of the team members who had made the errors were never mentioned except among the team members.

Over a period of about four years, there were two team members who did not pull their weight. They were given a couple of warnings. When they did not shape up, they were given a reasonable amount of time to find new jobs. Both of them eventually resigned.

The other members of the teams learned to work as a unit, covering for each other when necessary. One measure of their effectiveness was the way they tacked incoming phone messages on a centrally located cork board. Team members kept an eye on the board. If any member of a team was unable to respond to a business call within half an hour, for any reason, some other member would contact the caller to see if there was anything that could be done. This went a long way toward developing user confidence in the teams. Talk about being productive! These were outstanding teams.

Hurry-up Changes

There is no information systems environment in which hurry-up changes can be avoided. The information systems departments in place today support dynamic organizations. Changes are a way of life. Cost estimates made by veteran analysts to cover contingencies for modifications or enhancements to systems may seem excessive to the inexperienced, but veterans know that their estimates must account for the modifications that must be made in less time and with less manpower. In about eighty percent of the situations like this that occur routinely, changes are made, limited testing is done, and due to the skill and knowledge of the analysts, the changed system works properly. However, when such changes do not work, "Shifting the Blame" gets played in spades. In addition, there are long-term consequences such as those illustrated in the following story about Greg, a manager of fourteen analysts and programmers.

For almost a year, Greg's group had been performing exceptionally. Its members had implemented numerous small system changes and several major modifications, in less time than originally estimated. However, they had done this largely on their own initiative by working unpaid overtime—without even being asked! Greg tried to explain this to his immediate superior and then to the vice president of finance, his immediate superior's boss. He explained that the members of his staff had performed "above and beyond the call" when necessary, but that the performance of his staff would deteriorate if such calls became commonplace. All Greg and his staff got was more work. Greg was unable to lean on the analysts and programmers to produce more and more, and was eventually forced to resign. A few of his staff also resigned. The morale was not great among those who remained. Very few could be found at their desks after 5 o'clock.

Operating in the hurry-up environment is something that requires enlightened executives and information systems analysts and programmers. The executives need to know that they've got to provide relief from time to time. The analysts and programmers need to realize that from time to time there are going to be some unreasonable demands made. There's got to be a trade-off. If executives push too hard for too long, morale starts to slip. Overburdened programmers and analysts find ways to get back what they are being forced to sacrifice. The extra steps that could be taken, and would be taken in a more congenial environment, are not taken. Productivity suffers.

The Security Accessibility Trade-Off

While most software systems are developed to make it as easy as possible to access information, security systems and procedures are intended to restrict access of information to only those who need it. The trade-off involves productivity: the productivity of those who use the information, the productivity of those who manage and manipulate the information (the analysts, programmers, and database administrators), and the productivity of those who are responsible for safeguarding the information (the security officers).

Without describing the labyrinthine processes that can be put into place, we can say that the people who use the information stored in computer information systems will put up with just so much difficulty in accessing the information that they need. At some point, if access becomes bothersome, they stop using the systems that have been developed for them. Resourceful folks find other ways of getting the information they need. In doing so, they may resort to second-rate data. Productivity is impacted in two ways: First, use of second-rate data nullifies all the work that went into developing the systems from which it has become too difficult to get information; and second, working with questionable information from other sources requires that those using it must do more work, often significantly more, just to get it validated or into the correct format.

There are times when analysts, programmers, and database administrators have to perform functions that require access to information lying outside their normal needs. If security procedures are tight, they may not be able to finish their work. This is especially true when they are working off hours, which is an unfortunate necessity in the information systems field. Such situations often occur on weekends or late at night and may jeopardize the completion of a long series of tasks, or even worse, create a hurry-up situation such as one of those mentioned earlier. Effectiveness and efficiency both suffer as individuals scramble to circumvent the security procedures. All of this is unproductive. There are those who, when they encounter such a situation, get so frustrated that they call in sick for a day just to get over it. And so, another day is lost.

I once knew two security officers named Bob and Jim. They worked in the same shop but at different times. Bob was the kind of guy who worked with the users and the information systems staff to come up with a workable environment. Certain types of corner-cutting were allowed. If the vice president of finance, who was a stickler for security, had ever found out, there would have been hell to pay. But since going by the book would mean getting phone calls at all hours of the night or on weekends, Bob chose the risky route. Nobody ever blew the whistle on him. He made everybody's life easier; the users and the information systems staff just pretended that everything was the way it should be. In fact, just to make it look really authentic, they even complained about the security procedures every once in a while.

On the other hand, Jim wanted to play it safe. He was not a risk-taker. He just wanted to be sure that, if anything ever went wrong, it wasn't his mistake. Productivity decreased as both users and information systems staff members had to find ways to get around the cumbersome procedures that Jim had devised. Jim didn't last very long. Although he didn't make any big mistakes, he became so unpopular that he eventually resigned.

While I decry corner-cutting elsewhere, I recommend it here. A certain amount of corner-cutting is not only allowable, it is sometimes necessary. How much should be allowed depends on the situation. That's why this is called the security accessibility trade-off.

The Printer Paradox

There is no longer any doubt. Personal computers (PCs) have done more to bring computers to the people than anything else. Although to the novice some PCs are difficult to learn to use, most people put them to good use rather quickly. However, there is one aspect of the learning process that drives a nontechnical user up the wall: the printer interface. The following story about Ruth and Keith depicts what can happen.

Keith is a vice president of marketing in the recorded music industry. He is a nontechnician as far as computers go, but in his field he is respected by all who have worked with him. Ruth is an information systems analyst and an applications programmer. She is knowledgeable in applications but, like Keith, she is not a technician. Over the years, they crossed paths from time to time professionally and had earned each other's respect.

Ruth had taken the PC plunge in 1982 by acquiring an Osborne PC and a printer. Because she had recently learned of the peculiarities of printer interfaces, Ruth had the salesman at the store hook the printer to her Osborne computer to make sure that the interface worked before she left the store. This Osborne and printer turned out to be a wise choice for her for two reasons: First, the purchase was several thousand dollars less expensive than anything else available at the time; and, second, she was able to learn much about PCs and the software that went with them. Within several weeks, she had learned enough even to prepare her departmental budget with the spreadsheet package that came with the Osborne.

Keith's story is a bit different. In 1986, he acquired an IBM PC and a printer directly from IBM. Because Keith's application required letter-quality output, he bought a daisy-wheel printer, but he soon realized that there were other things than just word processing that could be done with the computer. However, these additional applications required higher-speed printing rather than letter-quality. On the recommendation of a friend, he ordered a non-IBM dot-matrix printer from a mail-order company. The printer came with a manual that to a nontechnician like Keith was indecipherable. Keith's duties as a vice president did not leave him a great deal of time to fool around trying to get the printer working, but he did try once or twice. The few times that he did try left him totally frustrated. He didn't understand the manual and, since he had gotten the printer by mail order, he really had no one to turn to for help.

In early 1987, Keith and Ruth caught up with each other at an interdepartmental planning meeting. During a short break, Keith commented on his printer problem to Ruth, and she so sympathized that at the conclusion of the meeting, she spent a couple of hours with the printer and the manual to try to get the printer working. As a last resort, she called another friend, a PC guru named Sam, and explained the situation. From the suggestions that Sam made, Ruth and Keith were finally able to get the printer working.

This story highlights another shortcoming of the simple high-tech solution to a problem. Here were two competent professionals faced with a situation that neither of them knew how to handle. Despite the fact that using personal computers is relatively easy, there are still some areas that require technical expertise. Taking time out to get help will save time in the end.

THE NIH SYNDROME

The not-invented-here syndrome can affect the attitude of either a group or an individual. Specifically, the NIH syndrome shows up as resistance to change that has been initiated by an outside individual or group. Like the high-tech syndrome, NIH is a mind-set; the people involved often aren't able to recognize their affliction. The resulting productivity leaks can cause lasting damage to a company. The following four scenarios illustrate different ways in which change can be undermined to the detriment of an organization.

Doomed from the Start

A few years ago, a manufacturing and distribution company acquired a database management system (DBMS) software product as part of its attempt to bring its management information systems (MIS) development strategy up to date. Instead of training its current MIS staff, the company initiated the hiring of some analysts and programmers experienced with the product. This was a mistake and it was a big one. The NIH syndrome showed up in the existing MIS, plant, and warehousing functions, causing much confusion and inefficiency in the company.

There was enmity between the newly hired group and the existing staff right from the start. Most of the new folks were recent college graduates with between two and four years' work experience, whereas many members of the existing staff were older and had more than ten years' experience. Members of the existing staff did little to help or encourage the newly hired MIS technicians. Although they tried to be friendly at first, the new members of the staff got the message.

The new staff began to develop manufacturing and warehousing applications using the new DBMS software. Some of the members of the group were quite polished and made presentations that were both impressive and frequent to the senior managers of the company. At the same time, few opportunities were missed to undercut the existing systems, the old MIS staffers, and the "hicks" in the plants and warehouses. Because of their recent training, much

of what they did was according to the book. They created specifications, diagrams, and charts; analyzed manual assembly procedures;
and performed structured-analysis-phase walkthroughs, exactly the
way they had been taught in their training seminars. Only when
all of that was finished did they begin to design and develop programs. This took several months. Everyone was impressed except
the old MIS staffers and the people who worked in the plants and
the warehouses.

In retrospect, what took place over the next year and a half could
best be described as a lesson in how to decrease productivity, while
demoralizing staff and wasting money. To illustrate, I'll use one team
and its project as an example. This team, made up of six analysts
and a charismatic (at least as far as being able to impress senior
managers) project leader, created a fundamentally sound system.
Once it was completed, they attempted to get it installed in one of
the company's plants. The project leader even had T-shirts made
up with "CONVEX IS COMING" (CONVEX being the system's acro-
nym) written across the front.

CONVEX never got off the ground. No one ever used the word
"sabotage," but it just seemed that the plant departments that were
supposed to support it and be served by it kept finding little things
wrong with it. There was an interface to another system that wasn't
included. There was a critical field missing from one of the databases. Some of the terminal devices in the plant could not receive
the screen display output. Every time some limitation showed up
in the new system, an individual in the plant and one of the old
MIS staffers were able to come up with something in one of the old
systems to take care of it.

There were numerous incidents like this. About two years after this company had set its new strategic direction, it was forced
to give it up. During the two years it was in effect, no new systems
were implemented, several old MIS staffers resigned, and the MIS
budget increased to four times what it had been. The DBMS software was blamed as the cause of the problem. In fact, the primary
causes of the productivity loss could be placed at the doorstep of
senior managers and the charismatic project manager. The project
manager did his homework and made masterful systems presentations. He had a reasonable answer to every question. The senior
managers were taken in because the project manager told them things

that they wanted to hear—that new technology, implemented by up-to-date technicians, would solve their information systems problems.

In this case, NIH was used by individuals who had been with the organization for a long time to counter the efforts of a ruthless project manager. Although understandable, it still stifled productivity. It could have been avoided.

Since implementing new technology generally requires some additions in personnel, there is a smart way to do it. Train some of the existing MIS staff to use the new technology product. Hire new MIS people, but at entry and junior levels. Train them to maintain the existing systems, and as they become more experienced, shift more of the existing MIS staff into the new technology. Not only does this enhance morale, it is more productive.

None of His Business

Marc was the director of sales services in the marketing organization of a company that manufactured and sold a line of relatively inexpensive products, whose prices fluctuated frequently. Marc's primary responsibility was to produce and distribute the catalogs for the line. His job was deadline-oriented and involved lots of last-minute changes. Marc was a bit high-strung and was known to be difficult to work with. Most of the time, the things paramount to him were the current catalog and the next fifteen minutes.

The fact that $2 million was being spent each year to produce these catalogs had not escaped the attention of Todd, the vice president of finance. He had Jim, the MIS director, assign Mary Jo, a senior analyst, to help Marc evaluate how a desktop publishing system could reduce costs. The only trouble was that Marc had not asked for the help, and did not want to get involved with desktop publishing. Marc's boss Paul, the vice president of marketing, did not get along with Todd and neither of them were what might be called pussycats. Mary Jo knew that the assignment would be viewed as encroachment on Paul's turf.

Mary Jo had some exposure to desktop publishing but had only a general idea of what it took to produce several catalogs each month. In order to obtain a better understanding of the process, she initiated several meetings with Marc. These meetings were fruitless, as Marc used them as a forum to moan about how difficult his job was, how he was understaffed, and so on.

Since Todd was becoming impatient with her, Mary Jo managed to talk Jim into assigning Nick, a junior programmer/analyst, to work with Esther, Marc's assistant. Both Nick and Esther were enthusiastic about the project and about getting desktop publishing into the department. Mary Jo called three vendors, gave them the specifications prepared by Esther and Nick, and asked them to prepare product demonstrations. Of the three presentations, one generated enough excitement so that word got back to Paul, who immediately became a fan of desktop publishing. It was now Paul's idea. Having crossed into Paul's turf by initiating the effort, Todd was now under pressure to deliver. Jim and Mary Jo had to add three other programmer/analysts. They were given three months to get the desktop publishing system implemented and to produce three major catalogs.

This story has a happy ending for Paul, Todd, and, ironically, for Marc; but not for Mary Jo or Jim. The system was installed eventually and has saved the company hundreds of thousands of dollars. Marc's job is now easier, he believes as a result of his own effort. In trying to overcome Marc's NIH, Mary Jo and Jim had let their other projects slip and were forced to resign. Although Paul got credit for the success, Todd at least had the satisfaction of knowing he was right. In the final analysis, Todd was correct in assessing the need for desktop publishing; however, his approach was of debatable merit, in part excusing Marc's resistance to change. But Marc's NIH indirectly cost a senior analyst and a director their jobs.

Pride That Kills

Once upon a time, there was a dynamic multidivisional corporation. Profits were exceptional, cash flow was excellent. At a time when almost all commercial data processing was being done in batch mode, a new flamboyant vice president of MIS persuaded key senior managers of both the corporation and the divisions that an on-line system would give them a competitive edge. Under a corporate MIS umbrella, a task force made up of both corporate and divisional technicians was set up to establish an on-line environment.

As with all pioneering efforts, there were difficulties, but they were overcome. The morale of the members of the task force was high. They were working on a leading-edge effort and their managers were supporting them. All in all, it took about a year and a half, but the efforts paid off. An on-line environment was established using a combination of standard and customized software that served the organization well for several years.

However, with each passing year the customized part of the software imposed increasing limitations on what could be done with new technology in the environment. Since all systems work has a life cycle, sooner or later even the most leading-edge technology becomes the trailing edge. It was no different in this operation.

The limitations that restrained the use of new technology became a major issue when one of the division MIS directors determined that a few of his major systems needed an overhaul. Basing his decision on feasibility studies conducted within his division, he elected to use the newly emerging database management systems technology to rewrite those systems. A study was performed by senior analysts from both his and the corporate staffs, and a DBMS product was selected—even though it would require either a new or modified on-line software support environment.

What took place over the next two years was a concerted effort, on the part of those who had set up the original on-line environment, to discredit the technology in general and the chosen software product in particular. Those who worked on the original effort now held middle and senior MIS management positions on both division and corporate staffs. Although they had every reason to be proud of what they had accomplished, they refused collectively to acknowledge that their environment was no longer up to date technologically and that it was time to make the transition.

Unfortunately for the organization, they were successful in their efforts. Both the technology and the selected product were discredited. The director who had advocated using it was eventually forced to resign over delays in implementation. The existing on-line environment was maintained at excessive cost to the organization for several more years until its limitations became such an issue that a couple of corporate senior managers got involved. Word had reached them from executives within the divisions that new technology products were not being used simply because the on-line environment could not support them. When they asked the question, Why not? they received explanations that they felt were double-talk. Not too long after that, there was a shakeup of the entire MIS organization and the on-line environment was revamped to support new technology products.

As this scenario illustrates, NIH can impede the course of necessary changes, changes that in the end will most likely prevail. Unfortunately, this company had to learn that through the great expense of hindsight.

Nobody's Tool

In the 1980s, battery-powered, hand-held computers equipped with limited amounts of storage, keypads, and scanners appeared on the scene. These devices can be used locally, to pick up and store information, and then, by means of a modem, to transfer it to a data processing facility.

A vice president of finance in a book publishing organization saw these devices as a way to improve the productivity of sales representatives. He thought that the devices could be used to take inventory in the stores that were visited by the sales reps. It was the vice president's idea that, once the bookstore proprietor had been shown how the device could be used in taking inventory, the sales reps might then be able to create orders on the devices and transmit them directly into the book publisher's order-entry computer system. The vice president saw this as an opportunity to increase the efficiency of his organization's ordering process and at the same time to help the bookstore proprietor.

The vice president of finance contacted the director of MIS and had him order two of the hand-held computers as a research and development project. He then contacted a vice president of marketing and ran the idea past him. His response was underwhelming. Undaunted, the vice president of finance decided to pursue the possibilities. He had the MIS director assign a senior analyst to the project. The devices were acquired and the analyst made a couple of trips to the field to see firsthand just how the sales reps operated. The reception that the sales reps gave the analyst was mixed, but there were a few who were enthusiastic about the possibilities. Within about three months, a preliminary system was designed and programmed.

For the next year, there was very little progress in getting the devices accepted by the marketing organization. The two sales reps who had been initially enthusiastic found that they did not have enough time to devote to testing the devices and the system. Most of the progress that was made came about because of the persistence of the senior analyst. The several marketing people who had become involved with the project kept avoiding a commitment to the selected device, and would mention two or three other devices that should be reviewed. The vice president of finance said that he could not afford the time to design and program two or three devices. One would have to be chosen and a commitment would have to be made to that device. The squabbling went on and on. The marketing people were upset that the project had been initiated by the vice president of finance and the MIS department, and would not cooperate unless they themselves chose the device that would be used.

About a year after the project was initiated, the senior analyst resigned to take a job as a project manager with another book publishing company. Two months after starting his new job, he asked a friend at his prior employer if he could borrow one of the hand-held computers for a couple of weeks. His friend lent it to him, and he was successful in convincing the marketing manager of one of the divisions of his new employer that the device had potential. After returning the borrowed device, his new organization acquired a few of their own. Within four months, they were successfully applied as both inventory-taking and order-entry devices. Productivity was dramatically enhanced because the devices significantly reduced errors and order-taking time.

COMMENTS

This chapter presented two mind-sets that impede productivity: the high-tech syndrome and the not-invented-here syndrome. These are subtle problems, like leaks, that will grow if they go unchecked. It must be recognized that high tech has potential, but in many cases it is not an automatic cure-all. Many organizations expect too much from information systems technology and the technicians who support it, hampering their own productivity. We must all be aware that, as technology changes, businesses must change; NIH threatens the survival of businesses, often leading people to block implementations that they eventually will be forced to make.

The cure for both syndromes is the careful guidance of management. The limitations of technology must be recognized and personnel should not always be held accountable for these constraints. Likewise, when introducing new technology, managers should actively seek the cooperation of the staff, rather than instantly demanding submission. Often, a little time and tolerance will, in the long run, save an organization a lot of resources, both human and financial. With this new mind-set, managers can fix the leaks in productivity that have already appeared and prevent new ones from occurring.

2

Using the Tools

What we have is a situation in which we are data-rich and information-poor. What we want are management information systems, but what we have are clerical information systems. There is no applications backlog: That is a myth generated by those who want to sell hardware and fill seats at seminars. Using our existing systems, we must effectively and efficiently use the data we have and the data we collect.

The productivity questions and discussions given in this chapter examine current and future ways in which information systems can serve management. Each section poses a question that, with its answer, will guide a reassessment of an information system's strategy. Management must be made aware of two realities: There are resources in most organizations that are not being fully exploited; and, there is technology on the market that is becoming more essential to an organization's productivity. Three steps must be taken to confront these conditions: First, with existing information systems technology, we can improve the quality and timeliness of the information that managers and executives need; second, by delivering the first, we can reduce managers' and executives' uneasiness with information systems technology; and third, once the uneasiness with the technology is reduced, we can introduce new technology in stages and further improve the quality and timeliness of the information. These three progressive steps then become a repeating cycle. This chapter points toward actualizing the potential of existing technology to better serve the needs of management.

WHAT PROBLEMS DO CONTEMPORARY IS SYSTEMS FACE?

In most contemporary organizations, the information systems (IS) area consists of a loosely integrated or interfaced set of applications that generally support day-to-day operational business functions. While clerical functions get the most from these systems, the first- and second-level managers only get some of the applications they need. The oldest of these systems are batch-oriented and use sequential files. Others, developed during the 1970s, are interactive, using direct-access or indexed files. Senior managers and executives get their information through written or verbal reports from the lower managers, rarely through direct use of the system. Because of the structures of the files and the orientation of the systems, most systems are unable to cater to all three groups of users.

Complexity

The systems are complex: A typical flow of data through a logistical business application includes input, validation, file maintenance, processing, and output. Systems may be batch or on-line or a combination of both. Improvements in communications software during the 1980s and the economics of using terminal devices have made on-line processing commonplace. Contemporary order-entry operations use dozens, even hundreds, of terminal devices to enter and validate orders for merchandise, to inquire as to inventory or customer status, to perform file maintenance, to apply cash receipts, and to perform numerous other functions.

Redundancy

In their current form, these loosely integrated systems are something less than marvels of productivity. They are full of redundancies, both in terms of the information being stored and in similar processes being run in parallel. There are reasons for this. The various functional systems were in all likelihood developed and installed during different stages and have been heavily modified over the years. It is, therefore, quite possible that a number of the accounting and financial applications may still be batch-processing oriented and are using sequential files, while more recently developed systems, such as order-entry, make use of communications software that supports on-line transactions against direct-access or indexed files.

Incompatibility

In many companies, manufacturing and marketing applications were developed last. Frequently, they were implemented as on-line transaction systems making use of communications software. In many cases, they used database management system software products with cross-referencing among files. All three of these levels of technology—batch/sequential, interactive/direct and indexed, and interactive/database with cross-reference—are essentially incompatible with one another. Integrating them requires a significant effort on the part of the information systems organization.

Despite all this, there are practical ways of creating integrated structures that can make organizations more productive. These involve spending some money up front, but do not necessarily require a heavy commitment to new technology products. As shown in Chapters Eight and Nine, there can be an eventual payback in the long-term savings and improved productivity.

WHAT DO MANAGERS WANT AND WHY CAN'T THEY GET IT?

First-line managers would like to see applications integrated and using a common set of files or databases so that reports and summaries would balance. Many first-line supervisors lament that they spend a lot of unproductive time reconciling reports and summaries that appear to be out of balance, having been produced by applications whose files are maintained independently and according to different schedules. Managers of functional areas would like to be able to interact with applications, to ask questions randomly and receive responses within a few seconds.

Senior managers and executives would like to have models that they could interact with, to ask the What-if questions. They would like to be able to get at yesterday's sales, first thing in the morning, on a workstation. They would like to be able to generate profit and loss statements on demand rather than waiting till the end of the month, for each profit center, product, or product type, or for some other major components of the business.

The desire that managers at various levels have for these reports or displays is understandable. The potential to produce them exists within the available technology. The complications arise due to lack of system integration (mentioned above), cost, incompatibilities in file organization, and inconsistent management styles, as discussed in the following subsections.

Cost-Effective Systems

When IS technicians or managers say something can't be done, they don't really mean it; what they mean is that the job will be difficult and, consequently, expensive. Often, IS technicians and managers are reluctant to make changes or modifications that appear simple to functional users. In the past, their time and cost estimates have frequently been second-guessed and they've had to implement changes and modifications too quickly. The justification for their apparently lengthy estimates included explanations that quick-and-dirty changes would lead to complications in the future. These explanations were often ignored and quick-and-dirty changes were implemented.

In many organizations, the future has arrived; many applications are polluted by the complications caused by changes made earlier. Thanks to this pollution, the response "that can't be done" comes closer to the truth now than it did in the past, regardless of cost. It is common knowledge that the cost of maintaining systems is quite high and those in the field know that past sins have contributed significantly.

Compatible Files

There is an inherent conflict between maintaining rapid input/output and processing activity for operational applications and creating up-to-the-minute summary information for strategic management systems. If an organization wishes to minimize the number of terminal devices that are used for operational functions, such as entering orders, applying cash, and responding to customer queries, it must develop and implement transactions that execute quickly. Fewer terminals are needed because quickly executing transactions require minimal input/output activity. Now, if an organization wants each transaction to update some summary database that provides strategic up-to-the-minute information to senior management, additional input/output activity is required. That increased input/output activity is going to reduce the speed of the operational transactions.

The conflict can be alleviated somewhat by leaving the operational transactions alone and having the strategic summary database updated in batch mode in the evening when the interactive, on-line portion of the application has been shut down. The management summary data is then one day old. If senior managers and executives can accept that, then the only competitors for computer resources are the operational transactions themselves and the queries entered by the senior managers and executives. The impact is minimal, but the information is not as current.

This particular issue is a critical one for senior managers and executives to understand. Policy should be set to prevent conflicts from arising among first-line, functional, and technical managers over which operating philosophy is to be used. With no policy, there will be hybrids, some applications mixing strategic management summary database updates with operational transactions and others going the batch route. This situation results in some strategic summary information being current and other summary information being a day old. It is just such an operating environment that leads all levels of management to believe that the technology is more of a hindrance than a help.

Consistent Management Styles

Changes in management have a potentially negative impact on the ability of the information systems organization to respond to the needs of all levels of management. Now, there's no doubt that changes in management are going to occur; I am not suggesting that this practice be discontinued. However, I must point out that there is an impact on the information systems function of which managers should be aware.

When a position is filled by an individual, that individual's operating philosophy fills that position also. When changes are made at the supervisory or functional management levels, the individuals involved attempt to impact the way systems supporting their function operate. Those supervisors and functional managers that occupy a position when an application is being designed and developed have a great deal to say about what it does and how it does it. If those supervisors and managers stay in their positions, they continually refine the application, a situation that is relatively easy for the information systems folks to accommodate.

If the supervisors of the functional managers leave their positions and are replaced by other individuals whose management styles are radically different, then it is usually more difficult for the IS function to adjust. The new supervisors or functional managers may want to make major modifications to the way the application functions, or they may even wish to capitalize on new information systems technology, complicating things even further.

Nothing is permanent, but the rate of turnover in senior management and executive positions is generally somewhat lower than in supervisory and functional management positions. Therefore, if an information systems organization is to design and implement strategic systems, the senior managers and executives ought to set the philosophy underlying these systems. In order to do so, it is recommended that they understand, in general terms, what is currently available and what is apparently going to be available in the near future through IS technology.

WHAT IS CURRENTLY AVAILABLE?

While technology offers solutions for many types of business problems, data processing professionals must know about the technology before anything can be solved by it. Managers should not only keep on top of new technology, they should take an active interest in exploiting the full resources of current technology. This practice will make technology investments truly cost-effective. It would waste time and money to wait for an application that is already feasible with a current configuration. In the section that follows, I discuss ways in which current technology—small computers, fourth-generation languages, and management summary subsystems—can be applied by managers for immediate productivity improvement.

Small Computers

Few would disagree that personal computers and the numerous spreadsheet products, word processors, and database packages have increased productivity throughout the business world. The amount of output, from analysts, typists, graphic artists, and others, has increased dramatically since these PC machines became generally available in the mid-1980s. This increase in productivity came about as people, some without technical training, took the initiative and learned to use an effective tool with relative ease. In doing so, they began to apply the technology in ways that had been thought impossible.

Taking the initiative with computers will help subordinates and executives alike. When subordinates take initiative and become more productive, executives benefit by getting greater productivity out of their subordinates; subordinates benefit as they increase their value by adding to their skills. Executives can help themselves by learning fundamental computer skills as well. Small computers can be used for an increasing number of applications, such as models and prototypes. Senior managers and executives wishing to utilize small personal computers should invest some of their own time in order to learn how to use them. This is not a radical recommendation; it has worked before.

In my own professional experience, I have seen situations in which executives have acquired small computers, have made the investment in learning, and have reaped the rewards. In one situation, the president of a division in a large corporation acquired an IBM personal computer and developed some BASIC programs to do a break-even analysis for a product manufactured by his division. This individual made an investment of his own time and was so pleased with the results that he ordered several small computers to be used in other functional areas of the division.

As a by-product of learning to use a small computer, executives also become computer literate, enabling them to understand both the benefits and the difficulties involved in working with computers, and to attain better insights as to what the information systems function can and cannot do.

Some of today's high-powered small computers are called workstations and are being connected to other computers, both large and small, in networks. To realize the full potential of PC networks and distributed processing, technical skills are essential. However, local processing is still possible with a nominal investment of time. By connecting PCs to mainframes and to each other, we can cause even greater productivity gains to be realized. This is discussed more fully later in this chapter, in the section called "Distributed Database Management Systems."

Fourth-Generation Languages

A fourth-generation language makes it possible to access data in a database without writing a program. However, this explanation tells only half the story. In order for a fourth-generation language to be used, a database that can be responsive to that language has to be set up. Once that has been done, the fourth-generation language can be used to access data in that database.

We've come a long way since the late 1940s and early 1950s when the only individuals who were able to interact with computers were the engineers and scientists who built them. By the late 1950s and early 1960s, what have become known as procedural programming languages were in use. These languages, such as FORTRAN, COBOL, and BASIC, were used by computer programmers who wrote a series of statements, called computer programs, that told the computer what information had to be retrieved and how to retrieve and display it.

In the late 1960s and the early 1970s, the arrival on the scene of database management systems technology (for setting up databases on single machines) set the stage for nonprocedural or fourth-generation languages. How to retrieve information is part of the specifications that the database administrators use in setting up the database. These languages, like small computers, are making it potentially easier for those without technical skills to access information stored in computers. Our tardiness in realizing the potential and the associated productivity improvements with fourth-generation languages was primarily due to the difficulty in setting up integrated databases.

For most organizations, it was virtually impossible to create integrated organizational databases until the late 1980s. There were two reasons for this, neither of them technical. First, it simply took a long time for everyone from the executives to the first-line supervisors to understand the value of an integrated database. Second, after the value of database technology was understood, it took a long time to actually perform the two-part process (designing database structures and transferring information from the conventional files into those structures) to convert the hundreds of conventional files into databases. Two later chapters, "An MIS Plan That Worked (for a While)" and "An Executive Starts His Own MIS," illustrate these difficulties as two executives see the value of integrated databases and put their ideas into action.

Management Summary Subsystems

The following paragraphs describe a system that is achievable, as opposed to available, with current technology. Simply put, management summary subsystems provide a way to get timely information to management.

Let's take a look at how most organizations work. During the day, many contemporary businesses support a number of interactive on-line systems. Through the use of terminals and workstations, data is entered as it arrives and queries are responded to immediately. Although there is some batch processing mixed in, the bulk of production batch processing is done on the second and third shifts. From approximately 6 A.M. until 9 P.M., one or more on-line applications are used for order-taking, file maintenance, responding to queries, supporting application program maintenance and development, and so on. This fifteen-hour span is sufficient to provide about twelve hours coverage for all locations in the continental United States. Late evening through early morning hours, say from perhaps 9 P.M. until 5 A.M., are used to back up on-line files and systems and to perform batch-processing functions.

In such environments, the batch-processing cycle produces reports that are distributed to various operating departments in the organization. If the operating departments are nearby, these reports are delivered by local messenger or trucking services. Otherwise, they can be transmitted electronically to printers located in the operating departments' offices. Some organizations require summary reports as well as detailed reports. The summary reports generally are for functional managers and executives while the detailed reports are used by first-line supervisors and their staffs. In a few organizations, summary reports are produced on workstation screens. Performing this function is one of the elements of a true management information system. What is surprising is that more organizations are not doing this.

I recall one organization in which a management information system was created using existing technology. The system was not what anyone would call an elegant implementation, but it was functional and is still in use; new components are continually being added. The system is menu-driven, so that executives and the others who use it are not burdened with commands that have to be memorized and keyed in. Once past the identification and password required for security, a user needs only a few menu-guided keystrokes to access the information. On selected workstation screens, by 5:30 each morning, the system initially provided four varieties of summary screens displaying the prior day's activity. In this management summary subsystem there were nineteen sets of workstation screens. Some of the sets included only one screen of information; others had several. One set provided gross sales, returns, and net sales, by day, month-to-date, and year-to-date, and from first-sale-date-to-date, for each product, a set of over fifteen hundred screens.

Behind the scenes, the system was conceptually simple. As part of the close-down process in each application, various summary totals were posted in sets of small files. As the totals were put in these files, the current date was also entered. In this way, there was always information available in the management summary subsystem files. In those cases in which delays were encountered, the information from an earlier day was still present, the idea being that one-day-old information was better than no information at all.

The system was developed with the technology available in the installation. The software to support the function at first was an on-line editor, known for its ease of use, if not for its efficiency in execution. However, making this information available to executives and managers made the effort worthwhile even if it offended the sensibilities of some information system purists. Since the system was constantly being enhanced, the inefficiencies of the on-line editor became more apparent as more summary screens were added. About two years after it was put into use, an effort was undertaken to convert the prototype to a conventional on-line system.

WHAT IS COMING?

I make no claims to supernatural vision. Foretelling the future is a risky proposition. Projections into the future are, at best, cautious extrapolations based on past and current experience. The extrapolations that follow deal with distributed database management systems and computer-aided software engineering.

Distributed Database Management Systems

Distributed database will be to the 1990s what database was to the 1980s. The technology to support a distributed database environment is beginning to emerge from organizations such as IBM, Cullinet, and ORACLE, among others. Realizing the potential offered by distributed databases will be complicated somewhat by the fact that there is no single, authoritative definition of what a distributed database is. I am not offering a definitive one of my own. I think it is best to let the dust settle. Yet, even with the lack of a precise definition, there does exist a general idea of what a distributed database is and of the value in developing software products to make it a reality. The organizations mentioned above are betting that distributed databases are viable.

Using the most general definition, a distributed database has its data stored and processed on two or more computers. At this level, distributed databases can be easily understood by executives, functional managers, and first-line supervisors. What is not understood, however, is the complexity of the software required to support a distributed database. This software, aptly called a distributed database management system, must have built into it the necessary programming to assure the security, integrity, and availability of each data element in the database; although the database is housed in more than one computer at more than one location, the system must be able to provide information to those requesting it in a timely and efficient manner. This kind of thorough full-function capability is not yet built into current distributed database system software products, but will become available in stages during the 1990s. In order to remain viable, organizations will have to move slowly, step by step, to realize the potential of this technology.

Although the technology to support a distributed database environment has only partially arrived, starting early will pay off later. Using cautious baby steps, rather than plunging in when forced to, can lower resistance to new technology. People are not as intimidated if the change is incremental rather than all at once. The learning curve, although longer, will be less pronounced; new material will be absorbed in increments and intermixed with hands-on experience, rather than in a large dose that must be absorbed quickly with little hands-on experience. Since distributed database technology is on the rise, efforts to adjust now will make the transition a more efficient step toward productivity.

Computer-Aided Software Engineering

Another technological development that promises to mature during the 1990s is computer-aided software engineering (CASE). CASE products are sets of tools that are designed to help (perhaps "force" is more appropriate) analysts to develop systems that are better documented and more easily maintained. The intended function of CASE tools is that they automate all stages of the systems development life cycle. This includes analysis, design, programming, testing, implementation, and maintenance. It would seem that the ultimate set of CASE tools would be able to generate and update documentation, as well as source and object code from specifications provided by analysts. While it will be a while before such complete capability exists, the CASE tools currently in use and those planned represent significant steps in that direction. CASE technology is part of a continuing trend to transfer labor-intensive software development activity and maintenance tasks from analysts to computers.

As happens with all new technological developments, there are a number of experts, often self-appointed, who give seminars and write articles. Although the CASE experts' ideas often overlap, there is little agreement on what the various CASE tools actually are. However, it is possible to give a general overview of what is available and an approximation of what is coming. Currently, there are five generic components. The first might be called a computer-aided management tool, used to assure that the information systems organization is developing applications that are appropriate to an organization's objectives and in line with its resources. The second is sometimes referred to as a computer-aided analysis and design tool. This tool is used to facilitate the capture and recording of system specifications. Third is the computer-aided programming tool, often integrated with the computer-aided analysis and design tool, which can generate program code and documentation from specifications. The fourth component is the computer-aided software maintenance tool, used to analyze existing code and to indicate the impact of proposed modifications. All of these tools are designed to work with the fifth component, called a repository, which includes a data dictionary that contains a set of common descriptions of files, records, fields, and systems functions. All of these components are actually installed on a computer and used through workstations to develop applications.

That CASE technology represents the potential to improve the productivity of analysts and programmers is beyond dispute. From specifications entered, the CASE tools can generate clean, bug-free structured code. That capability alone will save hours of program debugging time. In addition, CASE tools transfer to the computer the tasks of keeping documentation current, maintaining program source lists, file descriptions, and record layouts, and of keeping track of the relationships that exist among them. However, in order to be used properly, CASE technology has to be viewed as strategic. If the benefits of common file, record, field, and database specifications are to be realized, then they must be applied across the entire spectrum of an organization's systems environment. Not only would it be fruitless to do it any other way, it would also be too costly, since CASE tools are not inexpensive.

CASE technology has passed the infant stage. Cautious use of what tools are available is recommended. Their potential is too great to ignore.

COMMENTS

In many organizations, there is an absence of true management information systems, that is, those which provide executives with on-line access to current summary information. Some would say that technology is failing to live up to its promise. This was true twenty years ago, when the term MIS was initially coined. What was promised by management information systems was beyond the technology of that time. Much of the data that was needed was not stored in computer systems. This is no longer true. It is certainly not for lack of data or for lack of technology; there is more than enough of both to put some fairly sophisticated management reporting systems into place.

Why don't we have true management information systems? Perhaps management can't make up its collective mind what it wants. College systems courses and professional systems seminars teach that no major systems effort can succeed without the participation of senior management. I have seen through many years' experience that this is only partly true. The statement should say that no major systems effort can succeed without the participation of a committed senior manager.

Many managers have finally awakened to the fact that too many resources are being committed to maintaining operational systems for too little a return. The technology currently on hand to build management information systems and the technical talent required are available in abundance. What is needed to build a comprehensive management information system is a committed group of senior managers that can reach a consensus on what it is they want and a willingness to fund the resources necessary to build it. It won't be done overnight, but steps can be taken, implementations can be completed in stages with deliverable components installed a few at a time. It can be done that way. It has to be done that way. Cooperation is our only hope.

PART TWO
Effective Use of People

The thought has occurred to me that most individuals' productivity is a function of their well-being. There seem to be two extremes at which people's productivity becomes substandard: when they either are oppressed or perceive themselves to be oppressed, or when they become self-satisfied and complacent as the result of productivity achieved by the generation that preceded them. I believe that there is a great deal of room between those two extremes where a balance can be struck so that individuals can be motivated but not oppressed, contented but not complacent.

In Part II, I detail some of the reasons why individuals become less productive, and I make some recommendations as to how executives, managers, and the troops can cooperate more effectively to produce goods and services of higher quality. Part II will show how some things—like the influence of hot-shot salesmen—had been thought to be effective and efficient, but were in actuality sand traps and tar pits that constrained productivity.

The day of the hot shot is over. Hot shots don't improve productivity; all they do is promote their own advancement. The idea that managers should use fear to make people productive has been proven invalid. The overall conclusion reached is that we need to reintroduce candor and a certain degree of humility into the workplace.

It is time to cooperate with one another. Collectively, we cannot continue to support a system in which there seems to be a smaller and smaller number of big winners and a larger and larger number of those who can barely survive. But it is not too late. There are some things that can be done, if we are willing to sacrifice our self-sufficiency in order to survive.

What can we do? Let's first admit that we are flawed individuals. Perhaps we can then acknowledge that we need one another in order to create quality goods and services. The technology that we apply today has great potential, but it is complex. To realize the potential of that technology, we need to work together.

3

Self-Preservation

Productivity is a dependent variable. If a person is hungry, a promise of a meal will make him productive. If a person is well-fed, the desire to excel may make him productive. If frightened or insecure, a person will become defensive and his productivity will be oriented toward survival, not toward the production of quality goods and services.

There are some managers who promote anxiety, believing that fear is the great motivator and will keep productivity high. I disagree. Fear is a great motivator, but the productivity that is motivated by fear is oriented toward finding ways to survive, not toward activities that are primarily good for the organization. Executives would do well from time to time to "give a small pat on the head" to those who are consistently productive. I once worked for a man who was a fairly demanding superior. One night, after the completion of a significant phase of a project, he came over to me, reached out to shake my hand, and said, "Thank you." Somehow I felt that he really appreciated my contribution. I had worked hard for that man; from that night forward, I worked just a bit harder.

This chapter discusses the sources of stress and anxiety in the workplace. The first half describes the symptoms of an over-stressful work environment, danger signs that signal the need for management to foster a more cohesive, productive atmosphere. The second half of the chapter strips away many of the myths about managers that tend to hamper communication between subordinates and superiors and falsely bolster management with an image of infallibility. Managers at all levels and their subordinates will gain from a heightened awareness of the sources of stress and the myths that disrupt the workplace.

SURVIVAL BEYOND BASIC NEEDS

It is a commonly known fact that the primary motivating force in all individuals and organizations is survival. This instinct for survival enables us to respond to threats to our existence or well-being. Fear can play a key role, inducing us to evaluate a situation and to formulate an action plan, sometimes very quickly, to ensure our survival.

For the past forty years or so, we in the United States have almost totally forgotten about this basic instinct. We forgot about it simply because of the unprecedented prosperity in which most of us lived. Both organizationally and individually, we took our survival for granted. Fear of losing a job began to diminish as a motivat-

45

ing factor. In the late 1940s, the President and the Congress of the United States passed the Full Employment Act, and took on responsibility for providing jobs for all citizens. The resulting prosperity that we enjoyed made it possible for our employers to be magnanimous. Various personnel policies were established in large organizations that made it rather difficult to fire someone.

On top of that, for nearly forty years almost without interruption, there were jobs galore. Well-known social psychologists such as Maslow and McGregor developed theories that dealt with needs and behavior that transcended mere survival. Maslow wrote of a hierarchy of needs, whereby people, having satisfied their basic survival needs, move on to higher-level needs, such as fulfillment and love. McGregor spoke of Theory Y management, advocating individual initiative. He theorized that managers were to be motivators and coaches, encouraging and exhorting their subordinates to realize their potential. During the 1960s and 1970s, these theories were taught in our colleges and universities and also in motivational seminars given to managers and executives. These theories laid the foundation for many of those magnanimous human resources policies of major organizations. It was the consensus that once basic survival needs were met, individuals would be motivated to "do a good job." It was believed that the old idea of using fear as a motivator was outmoded and counterproductive.

Then, along came the 1980s. Ostensibly, all the higher-need motivational factors were still manifested in most organizations' human resources policies. However, what was really going on was a subtle switch back to the old motivation-by-fear concept. In fact, the subtlety was that the switch was taking place surreptitiously. The human resources policies of the 1980s still reflected the theories put forth in the 1950s, 1960s, and 1970s, but what actually began to happen was just the opposite: Benefits packages offered to the employees of large organizations looked good, but were actually nothing more than ways for management to cut costs. Furthermore, so-called golden parachutes being given to senior executives were among the most insidious productivity inhibitors that were ever invented. They protected those who required and deserved protection the least, cost U.S. corporations untold millions of dollars, and fortified the cynicism of those further down in the organizations.

During this same period, consolidation and downsizing of organizations were abundant. Individuals, sometimes numbering in the hundreds and even in the thousands, were laid off, fired, or forced into early retirement. Those managers and executives who consented to the layoffs did so in an effort to assure the survival of the organization. In many situations, it was necessary. In others, it was motivated by short-term greed.

Survival and Signs of Stress

People who feel that their future is threatened are not productive for an organization. They expend most of their energy trying to assure their own survival. "Hierarchy of needs" goes out the window. Productivity drops. Given this, managers and coworkers should be wary of the behavior patterns and attitudes that manifest themselves among people who are anxious and fearful:

- Some seem to celebrate when other individuals or groups fail. This behavior indicates a collapse of the cooperative attitude needed in the workplace.
- Some create smoke screens, speaking in half-truths and delivering cryptic explanations, attempting to cover up mistakes and avoid responsibility for problems.
- Others deal only with projects that will make them look good. They are so concerned about avoiding problems that they are hesitant to extend themselves for a less stellar but worthwhile project. This behavior not only kills projects that are good for the organization, it frustrates those who try to initiate them.
- Still others, having a need for continual attention and recognition, demand a majority of their superior's time. These people are either marginally productive or have a negative influence on productivity. These attention-getters should be given an opportunity to get up to speed. Failing this, they should be shown the door.
- Some create situations in which they make themselves appear indispensable, devising convoluted procedures for doing their job. For example, if they are supervisors, they become one-man gangs, doing the lion's share of the work while their subordinates do only the most menial tasks. If they are technicians, they attempt to control an area and

become its expert. Both the supervisors and the technicians who do their jobs in this fashion are unwilling to share what they know with others.

• Some are fearful of being conned, or tricked out of a promised agreement; they become the office cynics, finding sinister motivation behind every action. Such workers take great delight in broadcasting their commentaries to all who will listen. Needless to say, this does not enhance productivity.

When a good number of the troops and middle managers perceive that their survival is not assured, they channel their efforts into maintaining their survival rather than toward producing quality goods and services. This is counterproductive, as can be seen by the behavior patterns I have just described.

The business world is not unlike a battlefield: War is said to consist of long periods of mind-numbing boredom, punctuated with short periods of gut-rending fear. Boredom occurs among people who work at jobs they don't like, just so they can pay the rent. Although the information systems profession is among the most challenging and intellectually stimulating of fields, conversations with some analysts and programmers in private reveal their "quiet desperation" (as Thoreau put it). Although there of course is no real fear of being killed or maimed, there is the fear of putting one's source of livelihood in jeopardy.

I believe that if senior managers make some sacrifices and create a credible indication that they are more interested in producing quality goods and services than they are in feathering their own nests, the surviving middle managers and troops will follow suit. If the troops believe that those at the top are doing their part to increase productivity, they will respond. With such an incentive, those who actually do the work, and their immediate supervisors, will find ways to produce higher quality goods and services and, if they believe that they'll get some of the rewards, they'll do it more effectively and efficiently.

KNOW THY MANAGER

One source of stress for subordinates can be a faulty perception of their managers' image, capability, and motivation. Myths or stereotypes of managers often develop in corporate environments. Many of these are erroneous. A more realistic view of managers can be helpful in reducing stress, not only for subordinates but for the managers themselves. In this chapter, I establish some working definitions for two levels of manager. The first is the middle manager, an individual who has first-line managers reporting to him. The second is the senior manager or executive, who has middle managers reporting to him. This second group includes those in management positions all the way to the top of an organization.

Many individuals in both these levels of management experience the same types of stress that are felt by those at lower levels in an organization. They are as interested in self-preservation as anyone. In the past, it has not been socially acceptable for individuals, especially those in management positions, to admit that they are subject to anxiety, insecurity, and uncertainty. As a result of that consensus, it has been acceptable behavior for individuals to pretend that they are in control, self-assured, and assertive. This is how myths of management are generated. Perhaps the recent past and the current world situation have made it plain to us that we all, managers and subordinates, have reason to be unsure about the future. Expressing such concern simply reflects an honest assessment of the world around us. So let's be candid about our abilities, find ways to cooperate, and get on with improving our productivity. Let's begin with middle management.

The Myth of Middle Management

The ranks of middle management are filled with three types: those who have aspirations of becoming senior managers, those who actually like their current position, and those who are either hanging on or are trying to get back down among the troops. The middle managers with the aspirations are usually younger managers who are motivated to be productive in the hopes of being rewarded for pleasing their superiors. Generally, the older, more seasoned middle managers make up the other two groups and are motivated to be productive so that they can keep their jobs. At some point, every worker must choose a group to play this game, where the rules are flexible and not readily discernible.

The game can be rough. Middle management is that level of an organization at which competition is the most pronounced. There are many people in the lower levels; there are only a few in the upper. Middle managers who are attempting to advance perform their jobs only as far as it suits them to take the next step up. They do not expect to be in their current job for long and they act accordingly. In order to be successful, middle managers must exploit their subordinates while being exploited by senior managers. Competition is heavy in environments with little expansion and growth; upward movement of one individual becomes a threat to another. Although the most resilient and street-smart succeed, history teaches that it is difficult to retire from middle management.

The Myth of Senior Management

In writing this book, I have used the words "management" and "senior management" with discretion. The words, as used in books and seminars and among the academia, often imply some kind of united collective business acumen, directing organizational activities in an intelligent and informed fashion. This is a myth.

What I have found is that the words management and senior management are used to describe loosely structured groups of individuals with executive titles, all trying to impose their will upon one another. This is particularly problematic in systems development. Yet, without the involvement of a committed senior manager or a group of senior managers, whose sphere of influence is broad enough to cover the functional areas involved, the likelihood of success in developing and implementing a systems strategy is indeed marginal.

When a strategy is so vast that it requires the support of a senior management team, it can only succeed if that team is cohesive enough to last for the duration of time needed to implement the strategy. Senior managers only band together and act as "senior management" when there is more to be gained for all by doing it than there is to be gained by individuals for not doing it. And, since situations are fluid, individuals' evaluations on whether to play for the good of the team or for the good of themselves can change from day to day. If the good of the individual happens to dovetail with the good of the organization, swell; but if it doesn't, survival comes first. The golden parachute clauses that were found in the contracts of most senior managers and executives in the 1980s were ample evidence of where their priorities lay.

Senior Managers as Self-Assured People

I have noticed that there are many managers who aren't able to talk about anything besides business. Their self-assurance, so apparent when they are on their own turf, quickly diminishes when they are taken out of their element. Even at social gatherings, all they can talk about is what's going on in the office or organization. The narrowness of many such managers has had an adverse effect on productivity. Since there are numerous world events taking place and numerous ideas being expressed that can have an impact on every consumer market, I can't help but wonder about the soundness of decisions made by individuals with so parochial an outlook.

Often, managers with narrow perspectives are those who insist on having things done their own way. They usually are not interested in anyone else's point of view and they get theirs across by intimidating or shouting down the opposition. What causes some managers to act so unprofessionally? It goes without saying that they are concerned with self-preservation, but are they really self-assured? Or could their behavior be prompted by anxiety, insecurity, and uncertainty? With the complexity and capriciousness that exists in the world today, I for one am more comfortable with an individual who expresses some uncertainty than I am with one who is overly self-assured.

Senior Managers as Innovators

Most managers—albeit most people—like to maintain the status quo. Innovations, when they are made, often come about when they can no longer be resisted or come about through the efforts of a forceful individual who is aggressive enough to overcome the obstacles. Those forceful individuals who succeed are the ones who eventually make the covers of magazines. We rarely hear about those who fail.

Established managers do not like surprises and changes, and they usually do not like people who make waves. They have a vested interest in stability. Often, they are individuals who have a basic understanding of the way things *currently* operate; changes to that existing operation take away elements of their knowledge and consequently lessen their control. They too are interested in self-preservation and perceive their knowledge and control as necessary to survival.

I would suggest that the resistance on the part of many managers to innovations, such as having workstations installed in their offices, is based on fear. While using the excuse that they do not want to use a clerical or secretarial tool, the real truth may be that they are afraid of looking bad, that they are uncomfortable with computers and are intimidated by the arrogance of many technicians. This discomfort must be overcome.

Managers can increase their productivity by learning how to use workstations. They can also increase the productivity of their staff, by allowing staff members to do other work instead of responding to requests for information that the manager could easily get by pressing a few keys on a workstation equipped with a keyboard or a mouse.

Another aspect concerning the myth of innovation is the romantic idea that senior managers will reward aspiring young hopefuls who come up with new ideas for improving operations, for increasing sales, or for saving money. This is nonsense. Senior managers pay subordinates to do what they, the managers and executives, want them to do. If a new idea for improving operations, increasing sales, or saving money is to be forthcoming, the best that a subordinate can hope for is that the manager who implements it will remember where it came from and that he will pass along some kind of recognition or reward. When managers want to produce quality goods and services, and when they succeed in doing it, then productivity will be achieved.

Senior Managers and Power

In the movie *Butch Cassidy and the Sundance Kid*, there is an episode that illustrates the proviso that there are rules and then there are *rules*. In the scene, Butch's authority as leader of the gang is questioned by a man much bigger and stronger than he is. The big guy pulls out his knife and challenges Butch to fight to the finish—a winner-take-all showdown. Butch, knowing that he is no match for the challenger, slowly walks toward him and casually suggests that they discuss the ground rules for the fight. The big guy plants his feet apart and says incredulously, "Rules? In a knife fight? No rules!" However, Butch has disarmed him just enough to get off a kick to the groin. After that, it just takes one two-handed club punch to finish him off. The big guy had been right about one thing though: There were no rules.

Of course, in real life, there *are* rules. The difficulty is in finding out what they are and which set of them is in force at any given point in time. Those in power make the rules and enforce them in various and sundry ways. However, all power does not always reside in the hands of the senior managers. Frequently, power is in the hands of those who have information or who are in control of some vital operating function of an organization. Power is often in the hands of those who control *access* to senior managers.

There are times when a number-two person has as much or even more power than the number-one person. This power is acquired by screening the information that gets to the number-one person. Let us understand, however, that productivity is not the way to power. Having lived through several downsizings and having spoken to others who have had similar experiences, I know that it's not always those whose productivity is the greatest who survive the longest; rather, it is those who make themselves appear indispensable. Yet, truly productive individuals need not fear, for even though they may suffer some temporary inconvenience, they will eventually recover because they are productive.

COMMENTS

In this chapter, I have provided an informed opinion on self-preservation and how it is practiced in corporate America. To some degree, as we enter the 1990s, the anxiety level has diminished. Yet, we'll never be the same. Some say that the experiences of Vietnam, Watergate, and the 1980s have taken the romance out of America and have forced its inhabitants to view life more realistically. There is some truth to this notion. However, being realistic does not rule out being productive. We need to recognize things as they really are, and get back to work, working as hard as we can to be as productive as we can.

4

Sales Reps, Techies, and Consultants

Frequently, sales reps offer us solutions looking for problems; techies give us answers without explanations; and consultants are paid to learn from our experience.

A number of years ago, I became aware of a concept known as defensive driving. The idea was based on the theory that accidents could be avoided if drivers watched for the other guys and attempted to anticipate their actions. In this chapter, I present a derivative of that concept, which I call defensive management. The basic idea is that managers sometimes need to watch out for the other guys and to anticipate their moves and motives. They may also need to refrain from taking action or making commitments based on the recommendations of others. In many situations, the interests of those making the recommendations are not in line with those of the managers. In the sections that follow, I show how this is often the case with sales representatives (known as sales reps), certain types of technicians (called techies), and some consultants.

SALES REPS

Sales reps are put on this earth to sell. It is not their job to be helpful, only to make it appear that way. It is not their job to clarify, only to create an appearance of clarification. It is not their job to determine whether their product or service is best for a customer, only to convince the customer that it is the best.

Our job as customers is to make sure that sales reps serve our own best interests. We must be diligent that they do not waste our time and inhibit our productivity. In the following sections, I describe three ways sales reps waste our time and keep us from being productive: simplistic presentations, buzzwords, and hype.

Simplistic Presentations

When it comes to wasting time and making a large group of people unproductive for several hours or even for days, certain types of canned sales presentations take first prize. The larger computer manufacturers put on extravaganzas to announce new products or enhancements to existing products. Corporate executives and higher-level information systems managers invited to the presentations are subjected to product demonstrations that take place in the most contrived and controlled of all possible environments. Rarely do these presentations encounter any of the bugs that plague real-world computer centers.

Often, the presentations are slick, superficial, and flawless. At the conclusion of the presentation, the participants typically exchange stories about current sporting events or possibly some recent business dealings; it's all congenial and friendly and none of the important questions get asked. Nobody asks how these new products and features are going to be added to an already burdened computer center. Nobody asks what kind of conversion work will be required to interface these new products with existing ones. Those executives not from the information systems area go back to their offices expecting that installation of these new products will bring about flawless systems performance within weeks or perhaps, at worst, within a month or two. When they don't see that happening, they get upset.

How productive has all this been? If the sales reps make a sale, it's been productive and profitable for them and their organization. On the other hand, the presentation may have kept busy executives from accomplishing other productive work, and it probably has created expectations that may not be met. In the days to come, pressure will be put on lower-level information systems managers and technicians to recreate in the mud of a typical computer center what was demonstrated in a pristine presentation center.

So often I have seen a scenario that goes something like this: The new product gets ordered. A day or so later, it shows up at the computer center on a reel of tape; the systems programmer copies it to a disk and begins the process of setting it up and customizing it for his installation. A few minutes into the systems generation,* the systems programmer gets a query from the process asking what level of the telecommunications monitor is currently in place. The systems programmer keys in the response, say, Version 2.4. The gen process aborts and gives the message: INVALID VERSION OF COMMUNICATIONS MONITOR. Oops; then begins a process to find out how to get the communications monitor up to date. That gets fixed—best case, in a day or two, worst case, weeks later. Next, the systems programmer starts the gen again. He gets a bit further along but then finds out that a certain type of terminal device cannot be

---

*The systems generation, or gen, is the process that a systems programmer goes through to set up a new software product or an updated version of an existing software product.

supported with this new product and three of those devices are in the department that most desperately wants to use this new product. Oh Boy! Now some new devices have to be ordered, and on and on it goes.

Granted, this doesn't happen all the time, but it happens often enough to be troublesome; and when it does, it is extremely unproductive and very difficult to explain the delay to senior managers or executives who don't want to hear about releases and versions and devices that are not supported. They don't care about things like that. However, such occurrences give the technology a bad name. To avoid this, I suggest that canned presentations be looked upon with skepticism because the product presented by a vendor in a pristine environment is presented in an unreal situation.

Buzzwords

Buzzwords are the catchy product and feature nicknames created by marketing and media organizations. They are quickly picked up by techies and certain types of information systems managers and executives. They get bandied around and contribute to the general confusion and to the corresponding reduction in productivity, because few thoroughly understand what they mean. But in order not to appear ignorant, everyone starts using them.

Let's get back to basics. Sales reps use buzzwords to make an offering look attractive. However, the attractiveness becomes deceptive when potential buyers don't know what they're buying. They rely on their techies to evaluate the products, and there's nothing that some of these techies like more than new pieces of technology. Not all but far too many techies see these technology products as toys to be played with. When they get tired of them and see that they are not as terrific as they looked in the presentations, they cast them aside and tell everybody how bad they are and how other toys are better. They leave the landscape littered with these discarded toys and constantly cry for new ones.

Hype

Closely related to buzzwords is the marketing hype sales reps use to promote and sell new technology products. The short-term-gain mentality is also behind this: Make a sale now, get it into this quarter's bottom line. The media shares the guilt with marketing organizations in the generation of hype. In the information systems and computer field, the number of magazines, periodicals, and newspapers is impossible to count, but at the very least it is safe to say that there are dozens. The media industry also survives on hype, not only in advertising but in their journalism as well. Whenever a new piece of technology is announced, it gets immediate attention. It gets written up in every journal, sometimes in excruciating detail. When all is said and done about a new technology product, much more will have been said than done.

Sales reps understand that the purpose of hype is to generate interest. Marketing organizations and the media have common goals. Their survival depends on interest in new products. Marketing organizations use the media to make the buyers aware of their products. Succumbing to the quick-fix and easy-solution high-tech mentality of the times, some of the younger managers and techies, eager to get ahead, and some executives, misled by canned presentations, are more apt to believe the hype and acquire a new technology product than is an experienced veteran who has seen it all before. The experienced guy asks the tough questions: How's this product going to integrate with the devices and software in our current environment? What else do we need so that this product will work in our environment? Have the users seen what it can do? What do they think?

Believing the hype is like going for the setting rather than the stone. Hype is productive for marketing and media organizations; it contributes to their survival. If hype masks flaws and limitations, which it invariably does, it is not productive for the customers who acquire the products, for they must spend time and resources to compensate for the products' shortcomings.

The Bottom Line on Sales Reps

In most organizations, sales reps make their living by selling. Their income varies depending on quantities sold. Let's make the assumption that sales reps are no more honest or dishonest than the rest of us, but they differ in the sense that they can't count on a regular income the way salaried employees can. Their income is a function of their performance. Sales reps, quite naturally, are going to do things that will increase their income. First of all, they're going to try to find products that they believe they can sell. It is therefore not uncommon for sales reps to move around from one organization to another as they find products that they can more readily sell.

In larger companies, young sales reps may be *asked* to move to another organization once they encounter the overwhelming number of products they are required to sell. Often, it is virtually impossible for sales reps to stay on top of what all these products are and what they can do. They visit their customers, trying, with all the sincerity they can muster, to help. The managers in those companies want specific answers to specific questions. In most cases, the sales reps don't know the answers. To respond to the managers' needs, they offer either to set up a canned presentation or to send literature. No matter what the quantity of literature they leave behind, inexperienced sales reps leave managers wasting their time, flipping pages, trying to find answers to their questions.

Fortunately for us customers, veteran sales reps know how to please their customers. Seasoned sales reps will spend time with their customers and make attempts to plan ahead. While the time spent planning may not generate an immediate sale, it does enable the sales rep to position certain products so that a few months down the line, when the need does arrive, the sales rep is able to respond quickly to that need.

TECHIES

What the yuppie is to the financial profession, the techie is to the information systems profession. Information systems technicians come in all shapes and sizes, some truly productive, knowledgeable, and skilled; some reasonably so; and some outright frauds. The truly knowledgeable and skilled technicians and the journeymen technicians are usually both easy to work with and communicative. They are aware of the benefits of mutual cooperation. Fraudulent technicians give themselves away by their inability or unwillingness to communicate what they know. It is my belief that there is a direct correlation between the size of the ego of the information systems technician and how much of a fraud he is. The following sections elaborate on these observations.

Productive Technicians

There are some information systems technicians who are truly knowledgeable and skilled in their field, specializing in such areas as operating systems, telecommunications, database management, distributed processing, and applications. Technicians in these areas are extremely valuable. They are capable of dealing effectively and efficiently with complex technical situations. In situations requiring intense concentration, they may prefer working alone, but at other times, they are usually willing to teach others what they know. Although it is often difficult, they are generally willing to communicate in nontechnical language to their superiors. They have the confidence to say what they think and to teach what they know.

Journeymen Technicians

Journeymen technicians, in the right circumstances, will also be candid, acknowledging that they are aware of their limitations but helping in whatever way they can. In threatening situations, journeymen may become reluctant to cooperate since they may begin to feel insecure and realize that their technical knowledge is their primary key to survival. It is unfortunate that in today's business climate many of them feel threatened. These journeymen make up the majority of the information systems work force, and when they become reluctant to cooperate, productivity suffers.

Fraudulent Technicians

It is the fraudulent technicians, however, who really inhibit productivity. The discerning person can sometimes spot them by watching for certain behavior. The fraudulent techie with an oversized ego is thoroughly familiar with a particular piece of technology, either hardware or software, and insists that piece of technology is the best and that any and every other piece of equivalent technology is no good. His motivation is that his knowledge of this single piece of technology makes him an expert. He withholds information simply because he does not possess it; he is afraid that an admission of his lack of familiarity with other technology would make him look like less of an expert and would expose his limitations. Beware of the techie who bad-mouths a particular product, especially if that product has been around for a while. This type of fraudulent techie inhibits productivity by impeding an unbiased evaluation of what may be a better product or by poisoning the well of a product before an evaluation has ever been made.

The Bottom Line on Technicians

We live in high-tech times. While I believe strongly that there are a number of improvements to be made in productivity that do not involve technology, I also believe that we need technology and technicians. What I am against is the level to which we tend to elevate both the technology and the technician. Technicians are nothing more than individuals like the rest of us. They have aptitudes and skills that give them value and the ability to do some things that others cannot do. However, it's a two-way street. Technology is not an end unto itself; it needs to be channeled into the effective and efficient production of quality goods and services. The direction to do that is generally provided by managers and executives. By uniting the efforts of the technician and the manager, we can improve productivity.

CONSULTANTS

In today's world, individuals calling themselves consultants are in heavy use. My experience indicates that we would do well to pay attention to what Robert Townsend has to say about institutional consultants. In his book *Up the Organization*, Townsend defines consultants as "people who borrow your watch to tell you what time it is and then walk off with it."* The following sections discuss four types of institutional consultants: arbitrators, hatchet men, technical fire fighters, and professional fire fighters.

Arbitrators

There are times when senior managers find themselves in disagreement about what should be done. They just can't seem to reach an agreement. In order to resolve the situation, they bring in institutional consultants as arbitrators. These guys are the watch-borrowers

---

*Robert Townsend, *Up the Organization* (New York: Alfred A. Knopf, 1970), p. 104.

Townsend refers to. The consultants who come in on these assignments are often quite disruptive. They don't understand the business, so they have to ask the people who do know the business to describe it to them. Many consulting firms will use their entry-level people to learn about the client's business while billing the client for an experienced consultant. I have met with these consultants and have helped them with basic skills having nothing to do with lack of industry knowledge but rather with lack of basic business knowledge.

The consultant-arbitrators go through a process that is merely an extension of the political skirmish that caused them to be called in the first place. The consulting firm's job is to determine who is likely to win the dispute, to find out what position that person favors, and then to put together a proposal that justifies that position. Usually, the winner is the executive who decided which consulting firm would be chosen. This is what Townsend calls the "telling what time it is" phase. Then, when it's all finalized and accepted, the consulting firm leaves with knowledge that it didn't have when it came in. This, of course, is what Townsend calls the final "walking off with the watch" phase.

Such consultations interrupt and disrupt current operations in the organization. They do so in two ways: first, by disturbing people who are trying to do their jobs; and second, by starting rumors that lead to rampant controversy in the organization. To state the obvious, productivity goes down as the controversy heightens.

Hatchet Men

I was present at the dismantling of a media conglomerate. I had worked there for more than twenty years. The man who was in the process of taking over hired a firm of consultants to come in to evaluate the various functions within the organization. Within a short period of time, these consultants became known as the "thirty percent boys." Each function that they visited usually wound up with about a thirty percent reduction in staff. One complete operating group and its divisions ceased to exist as its inventory and operations functions were sold to another corporation in the same line of business. A second group and its divisions were sold off. The remaining group and its divisions and the corporate structure were streamlined.

The individual who took over undoubtedly made a lot of money. Some say that he did so on the broken careers of people who had really been proud of the old organization and had enjoyed working there. The consultants were used to bring about the changes. The company went from being a number-one company in the entertainment business to being just another business with dirty carpets on the floor.

Technical Fire Fighters

Technical fire fighters are perhaps the most productive of all consultants. I have been involved with consultants of this type on several occasions, and for the most part, we have been successful. The chances for success in this area depend on the size and duration of the project—the more specific the task, the greater the chance of success. While working in a database management systems support function, I used systems software programmers as consultants to perform very specific tasks. In each of these situations, success was one hundred percent. The secret to the success was twofold: First, I had individuals on my staff with sufficient technical expertise to thoroughly screen the candidates for the consulting position; second, the tasks were very specific and of limited duration. I asked for and was given estimates; they were met and everybody won. All around, productivity was achieved.

Some projects were not so successful. In the first of these situations, I was given a technical consultant with impressive credentials, but who proved to be an ineffective worker. He suffered from that well-known disease called "incompletitis." This guy just couldn't finish anything; he kept refining things, but never seemed to be able to put the whole thing together into a working component. His project was a satellite system that we were trying to develop for the CBS News elections system. The thing never came up on Election Night, but since it was a secondary system, we got along without it.

The technical consultant offered numerous excuses for his failure, and I had to acknowledge that I had not given it the proper attention because of more pressing priorities. The payoff on this effort was that we learned to insist that specific milestones be achieved in certain time frames. Two years later, when the same thing appeared to be happening again, the consultant was dumped and a new one was hired. It was painful and we had to settle for less than we wanted because of time constraints, but on Election Night, we had a working system.

Another situation involved an individual who turned out to be a fraud. Hired to write a communications interface for an on-line application, this individual was clever enough to get through the screening process. It took about four months to discover that no progress at all had been made. However, this individual had been crafty enough to code several driver programs to create the illusion that progress was being made. It wasn't until about two months before the deadline that the fraud was discovered. He was fired and the project turned over to another consultant, who managed to get it completed on time, but the experience was unnerving.

Although technical consultants are generally the most productive, there are enough exceptions to warrant caution in their selection. There are no guarantees, but the best way to assure success is to make the task as specific as possible, and to deal with consulting firms that have a proven track record in supplying such skills. It is advisable to ask for and to check references. When checking references, ask if there is any perceptible weakness in the candidate. Even the most competent of us has flaws, but it's best to know what they are ahead of time rather than finding out later that an individual has a limitation that may jeopardize a project. On several occasions, I did this and found out things that helped me to avoid further unsuccessful and unproductive situations.

Professional Fire Fighters

Some time ago, I worked about four years as a consultant. Two occasions stand out that gave me personal insight into the ways in which consultants are used. The first situation occurred in 1975, when I was assigned to assist a small manufacturing organization in setting up a minicomputer turnkey system. The system was designed to support several functions, including inventory, forecasting, order fulfillment, billing, and the feeds to the accounts receivable and general ledger systems. When given this assignment, I went to my boss and admitted that I didn't have any background in manufacturing and forecasting and that my last exposure to accounting systems had been ten years earlier. He looked me square in the eye and told me that, at $30,000 a year, I couldn't say that. That was all he said. So, I went.

By asking questions in such a way as not to expose my ignorance, I managed to pull it off. Calling upon the knowledge and experience that I did have, I was actually able to make a few contributions to a situation that had deteriorated because of lack of experience on the part of the people who were installing the system. They were just a couple of young computer programmers who had found themselves thrown into a situation not of their own making, just like me. Since they were younger and even less experienced than I was, I was able to emerge as something of a minor hero.

In another situation, a few months later, I was sent to a small technical/vocational school in Pennsylvania to advise the school administrator on whether he should upgrade his existing computer configuration to a more powerful one. When given the assignment, I had never even heard of the computer in question. At this point, I knew better than to say anything to my boss about what I did and didn't know. So the next morning, I just got in my car and left. When I got there, I met a gentleman whom I'll never forget. He was an old-timer, holding this job until he could retire, but he took the job seriously. A man of great integrity, he wanted to do the right thing. He did not want to spend the school's money on a new computer if it was not needed. He was an "ol' country boy" who felt that maybe he was being "city slickered" by the computer company. Within an hour, I knew all that I needed to know about the situation. He explained it perfectly. I was there to be a sounding board. I didn't need to know anything about the particular computer.

Watching this old-timer operate was one of the highlights of my career. We had dinner with the computer company salesman, a young hot shot on the rise. This old-timer cleaned the rep's clocks. Occasionally referring to me as his advisor from New York, he had that sales rep talking to himself when the evening ended.

I returned to New York just a bit wiser, having seen how effective the old-timer was. My time with him was productive. Not to get a new computer at that time proved to be the correct choice. My boss was pleased with the results of the trip, since the climate at the home office was not conducive to getting new equipment either. My only regret was the thought that, given our idolization of youth, we're pushing people out the door at fifty because they're "too old." Certainly that school in Pennsylvania benefited from having such an old-timer as administrator.

The Bottom Line on Consultants

I have observed some consultants who took themselves and their consulting jobs very seriously. They seemed to believe that their wisdom was superior to that of those who had worked in an organization for years. These consultants stirred up all kinds of controversy and caused organizational damage and disruptions that took years to get over. When I reflect upon it all, I find that I am very skeptical about "experts," who are really just people who know a little bit more about something than others for a while. I use myself as a criterion to measure others: I've got more than thirty years' experience; I've written six books and some fifty professional articles; I've taught and lectured; I've developed and implemented systems both at a managerial level and at a hands-on level. Yet, I'm not overly impressed with myself, so why should I expect others to be? I just enter a situation and do the best I can. Sometimes I do well, other times I don't do so well. That's all anybody can be expected to do: their best.

The point of telling the two stories and relating my feelings on experts is to indicate that consultants are not always what we might expect. Consultants are used when executives want to get something done but do not want to take the responsibility. They hire consultants to come in, study the situation, and then make their recommendation. If the recommendation does not conform to what the executives want, the consultants can be sure that they won't be called back any time soon. Contrary to what one might think, improving productivity is not always what is being sought when consultants are hired.

COMMENTS

The purpose of this chapter is to advocate defensive management. In it, I have developed concepts and recounted experiences that are intended to motivate managers to embrace the concept. With few exceptions, sales reps, techies, and consultants do not contribute greatly to an organization's productivity. In fact, they often dilute productivity. This is only natural. Sales reps are in business to sell; they will only attempt to contribute to a particular organization's productivity if it is in their best interest to do so. Technicians are needed to solve problems, but they often cause problems by hoarding information or being fickle with technology. Consultants are also in business to make a profit and to improve their own capabilities as consultants. Their interest in an organization's improved productivity is greater when it ties in with what is wanted by those who hire them.

5

The Young and the Old

When I was a boy of fourteen, my father was so ignorant I could hardly stand to have the old man around. But when I got to be twenty-one, I was astonished at how much the old man had learned in seven years.
— *Mark Twain*

It's all that the young can do for the old, to shock them and keep them up to date.
— *George Bernard Shaw*

Good judgment comes from experience, and experience—well, that comes from poor judgment.
— *Anonymous*

There are several ways to categorize groups; a common one is by age. In the work force today, there are three age groups: people in their late teens and early to mid-twenties; those in their late twenties, thirties, and early forties; and those in their mid-forties and older. The focus of this chapter is on the first and third groups: the young people and the older folks or seniors.

At first glance, the characteristics of the two groups appear to be quite different, but a closer look indicates that they are also functionally complementary. In general, the characteristics of young people include enthusiasm, impetuousness, a desire to make things better, impatience, the willingness and the desire to accept and implement new ideas, a touch of apprehension, and perhaps an inflated view of their own importance. Generally speaking, the older folks tend to be laid back, deliberate, often reluctant to change their ways, patient, wanting to enjoy the fruits of their labor, self-confident, and aware of their limitations. In the current economic climate, individuals in both these groups are having difficulty finding employment. The reasons for the unemployment differ, and I believe that, because of these differences, individuals in both groups can complement each other.

THE YOUNG PEOPLE

Young people can serve as an inspiration to the older folks. Their enthusiasm and resilience revitalize older people who work with them. They can also help by doing some things faster and more efficiently. In my opinion, they are also wiser than their counterparts from past generations. Young people today are exposed to information from books, magazines, television, and radio. Events taking place around the world often are broadcast within an hour of their occurrence. This was not unexpected; Toffler and Naisbitt* told us it was coming. Today's young people are the best informed group of their kind in all history.

---

*Alvin Toffler's *Future Shock* (New York: Random House, 1969) and *The Third Wave* (New York: Bantam Books, 1980), and John Naisbitt's *Megatrends* (New York: Warner Books, 1982) forecast the increases in the quantity and speed of information.

An Informal Interview

What do young people see when they look to the future? Well, it depends on whom you ask. I talked with Glen and David, each 19 years old, and Nicki, age 22. Glen and David were college students who were working during the summer between their freshman and sophomore years; Nicki had just graduated from college and was working part-time while interviewing with publishers in New York City for a full-time position as an editor. All three of them were doing data-entry work; David held a second part-time job when he wasn't doing data entry. They were all hard workers and were extremely conscientious and productive.

I asked them how they viewed the future—college, their short- and long-term prospects—and how they thought they might benefit from the older generation. I found out that they all were concerned about the environment and the economy, especially the U.S. government deficit, and that they all thought college was important. When I asked whether they thought there was anything of value to be learned from people over forty, Glen and David both indicated that they didn't think about it much, although Glen said he learned a lot about being effective from watching his boss. They jokingly added that apart from an overall concern about the environment and the economy, their primary thoughts involved only the next two or three days.

Nicki said she was learning what not to do by watching an older person exercise what she believed was bad judgment. She told me of a friend whose father had been laid off from a middle-management job and had spent two years unsuccessfully trying to get a similar job. She added that she thought he should be trying to find something else instead.

Besides what they *told* me, these three young people showed by their behavior their commitment to doing a good job. They practiced being productive.

A More Formal Look

During recent months, print media coverage and TV specials have focused on young adults. A recent cover story in Time magazine* contained some interesting observations and revelations:

*David M. Gross and Sophronia Scott, "Proceeding With Caution," *Time* (July 16, 1990), pp. 56-62.

- Fifty-three percent of those polled said they are worried about the future.
- They are less interested in careers than the generation that preceded them.
- They want constant feedback.
- They are consummate game players and grade-grubbers.
- They prefer short-term tasks with observable results, such as cleaning up a park or teaching literacy to under-privileged children.
- They are skeptical when recruiters talk about long-term job security.
- They view teaching, long disdained as an underpaid and underappreciated profession, as a hot career prospect.
- They believe that the 1990s' economy will make a college degree a necessity.

According to the article, today's generation of young adults is small enough that the nation may face a severe labor shortage in the coming decade. A sanguine view of today's young adults sees in them a sophistication, tolerance, and candor that could help repair the excesses caused by the rampant individualism so characteristic in the 1980s. Money is still important, but crass materialism is on the wane.

These qualities were evident in their own words. A young lady from Portland, Oregon, was quoted as saying, "We are the generation that is going to renovate America. We are going to be its carpenters and janitors." From Knoxville: "We expect less, we want less, but we want less to be better." A young man says: "Kids aren't stupid. The Stones aren't playing rock 'n' roll anymore. They're playing for Budweiser." Another added, "I'd *like* to be an overachiever, but I decided I'd rather have friends than grades."

From these informal and formal sources of information, I detect a desire on the part of today's youths to get back to basics, to eschew the greed and short-term financial gains that were goals of the yuppies of the 1980s. Today's youths want to work on manageable tasks; they believe in teamwork and cooperation. It seems that we now have two groups that share common objectives and outlooks; perhaps the older and younger generations can join together

AGING: Some of the slowing down, the "not being able to do the things that we could do when we were twenty-five," is the down side of getting older. None of us likes to deal with it; we don't like to be reminded of our mortality. However, there is a flip side: There are a host of things that fall under the heading of experience that begin to occur to us as we get older. Having lived longer and seen and experienced more, we've learned to temper youthful enthusiasm with a certain amount of restraint. Our interactions with others have taught us to be a bit more tolerant and patient. We have entered into numerous interpersonal transactions and have become more discerning and, dare it be said, a bit wiser. It is this experience that we have to offer to business, the community, and to our young people.

to restore productivity. Let's turn now to some of the problems and possibilities that many older folks are facing.

THE OLDER FOLKS

The primary attribute that older folks have to offer is experience. However, most of those who want to return to the work force are going to have to be willing to share their experience while making considerably less in terms of salary and benefits than they had been accustomed to receiving. At the same time, businesses and government are going to have to realize that it costs less to pay people for working than it costs if they don't. While it's uncivilized for us to just let people lose their homes and starve to death, those of us who are working cannot afford to pay the bills for those who are not. The only way out of this dilemma is for experienced people to work for less and for business and government to hire them. Their own productivity and that which they can foster in young people will make this an investment with a payback.

A Wasted Resource

A valuable and productive resource is being wasted. Many men and women are actively seeking work, but remain unemployed primarily because they happened to get caught in a takeover or a downsizing. Though much of this downsizing may have been necessary, it has had a negative effect on productivity. While layoffs and firings may produce short-term monetary gain for the organization, the productivity of those let go is lost. These people have talent and skills, which cannot be put to use unless they can find some gainful employment.

The Over-Forty Crowd

The loss of a job is especially damaging for an age-group that has a more difficult time getting rehired. Let's call them the Over-Forty Crowd. For a couple of legitimate but purely economic reasons, those under the age of forty have an easier time of finding new jobs. Younger people can usually be hired for less money than those over forty, and their benefits cost less because they are less of a medical risk. This kind of hiring practice may not get high marks for compassion, but nevertheless, it makes good business sense.

As ruthless as it might sound, some downsizing of the American organizations of the 1980s was necessary. What we need to come up with now is a way to salvage a lost human resource—valuable experience and talent—without putting an economic burden on business. To make any kind of business sense, we've got to make it just as economical to provide work for those over forty as it is for those under forty.

Before looking at specific proposals for bringing workers back into the work force, we need to describe who makes up the over-forty group. For the purposes of the proposals presented below, let's say that men and women who reach forty—an age selected

> **RETIREMENT:** Who says we have to retire? I have, over the years, come in contact with men and women, some of them in their seventies, who do not wish to retire. They try it, but soon become bored, and begin to look for work again. Some, usually those who are able to afford it, try volunteer work. Others try to find gainful employment. Could it be that there is something inside some people that makes them want to be productive? If there is, what a waste it is when individuals are put off to the side just because of their age.
>
> Where did this idea about retirement come from anyway? A little research reveals that in Old Testament times, provision was made for the Levites to retire, but they were the only ones with such a provision among the twelve tribes of Israel. A bit more research reveals that the first modern proposal for retiring at a specified age, sixty-five, came about in Germany in the late nineteenth century. The idea, and even the age, was picked up by the United States in the 1930s when Social Security was instituted.
>
> Those who wish to retire, who have saved their money and have enough to live on, should certainly be allowed to retire and to enjoy themselves as much as they can. However, those who wish to keep on working should not only be allowed, but encouraged to do so.

arbitrarily as a place to begin—fall into five broad groups. The first group is made up of those with extraordinary skill and dexterity, those who either will never be fired or laid off or, if they are, will quickly bounce back and land something as good as, if not better than, what they had previously. These are a distinct minority and include people like H. Ross Perot, Lee Iacocca, and Bob Hope. The second group is made up of the doctors, dentists, teachers, lawyers, writers, playwrights, show-business personalities, and even some consultants and entrepreneurs who have enough of what it takes in either credentials or connections to get going again almost immediately.

A third group is made up of those who wish to remain on the fast track. They thrive on the competition and pressure of the corporate environment, and they wish to continue more or less as they are. In the fourth group are those who are looking forward to a full-blown retirement. They seem to have the right combination of street smarts and natural ability to do a reasonably good job without making waves. They have managed to hold on to their jobs and are in no immediate danger of losing their current income or their retirement income in the future.

Finally, there is the fifth group—those individuals who want to remain productive, but who can't seem to get back into the work force. The people in this group want to continue working in some capacity, perhaps even part-time, understanding that their income and benefits package may have to be less than what it had been.

The first two groups are fairly buoyant; their resiliency sustains them through hard times. But members of the third and fourth groups may join the fifth group at any time, either voluntarily or involuntarily. To stay in the fifth group requires an attitude change. *Those in it must be willing to settle for something less than what they had, at least initially, and must also be amenable to a change in what they do for a living.*

THE PROPOSALS

The following proposals are meant to stimulate the utilization of young people and older folks in the work force. Each proposal differs in its main orientation. Some are oriented more toward the former, others toward the latter, while still others concern both groups. In some cases, these proposals have been tried and have met success.

The rest are suggestions that I believe will prove effective, although to the best of my knowledge they have not been tried before. The proposals are: Internships; Youth and Experience on the Same Team; Using the Older and Experienced as Teachers; A New Approach to Part-time Employment; and Forty Plus: A First Step.

Internships

One way to introduce the value of productivity to young people is to offer them the opportunity to learn by working. I worked for a while with Tom, a college student who was part of a cooperative work-study program through his university. The program specified that students spend six months of each year in the classroom and the other six months working in business or industry. Tom was a sharp and dedicated intern who was liked and respected by everyone he met. His productivity was high. When he finished college, he went into the family business, the operation of a successful chain of computer stores. Because of Tom's headstart in business, he was able to be immediately productive in the family business. Tom was an example of the kind of young person that organizations should take under their wing. That organization, at little cost, made an investment that meant invaluable experience to Tom, and at the same time benefited from his productivity.

Another intern program I was involved with occurred during the summers of the mid- and late 1980s. CBS Records ran a program in which each year four minority students were provided with summer employment as interns in the MIS department. It was a program that was closely monitored. The students were required to maintain a certain level of academic achievement in order to qualify for the program. They were exposed to a real-world situation and they responded well. Everybody won. The students made the most of the opportunity and CBS Records' MIS department got work done that would have gone begging had they not been there. A few of the students returned for more than one summer. Three of them accepted full-time jobs with CBS Records' MIS department when they graduated. These individuals are still with the organization and are doing well. This program was continued for several more years, but was discontinued when the economic climate turned soft. It was a mistake to stop it.

Youth and Experience on the Same Team

There are probably many people over forty who would enjoy working fewer hours even if it meant making less money, especially if the choice were offered as an alternative to being fired or becoming a victim of downsizing. In fact, there are a number of tasks that need to be performed in the information systems field alone that an individual over forty might gladly do rather than be retired. One example would be the performance of such tasks as systems testing or documentation. Younger people much prefer doing the analysis, writing the programs, running some limited tests, in short, getting things going about eighty percent and then moving on to something else. Most older, experienced information systems analysts, or perhaps even an executive, understand the value of systems testing and documentation, the final twenty percent of finishing a job right, and would be willing to participate in the process.

Doesn't it make sense to give older persons a shot at a job like this, rather than pushing them out the door? Imagine a project team made up of three or four young technicians and one or two older, more experienced former executives or managers. The difference between this team and most traditional teams is that the older members work fewer hours than the younger members, perhaps totaling three or four days a week. Their pay might be one half to two thirds of what it was when they were executives or managers but they are still productive. In addition to doing the work, they would also be there to share their experience with the younger members of the team. I know this is radical, but isn't it worth thinking about? Isn't it better than putting a talented, experienced individual out on the street? The economic justification will be realized in the long run.

Using the Older and Experienced as Teachers

Not all unemployed information systems managers and executives have the skills necessary to be teachers, but those who do might be re-employed as teachers. Perhaps in-house seminars could be set up with the older managers and analysts presenting case studies that reflect real-world situations. Half-day classes could be conducted one or two days a week, perhaps one on company time and the other on personal time, exhibiting commitment on both sides, and the younger information systems analysts and programmers could attend and interact with the older managers and analysts who would run the seminars.

A New Approach to Part-time Employment

For a while during those more prosperous decades of the 1950s and 1960s, there was talk of reducing the workweek to thirty hours. At that time, people thought we could work fewer hours for the same pay and benefits. The idea came and went for a number of reasons, the primary one being that it was toward the end of that period when our national productivity began to slip. However, many small businesses and some innovative large companies have put this concept into practice—but with a slightly different twist: How about a shorter workweek for proportionately less pay and benefits? How about two people doing a job, each working three days a week, with a one-day overlap? One person could work Monday through Wednesday and the other Wednesday through Friday. In the right circumstances, doesn't it make sense to have two people each working at $30,000 a year than to have one working at $60,000 and the other unemployed? Won't we all benefit from this?

Clearly, these new ways of utilizing personnel are not right for every business. There are those who are inclined to keep working as they have been. I do not recommend disturbing this. What I am advocating is that, instead of laying off or forcing into early retirement those who wish to continue working, we should try some alternatives. Where is it chiseled in stone that the thirty-five or forty-hour workweek is an absolute that cannot be violated? Who wins when major organizations lay off thousands with expensive separation packages? Layoffs cost the organizations; the organizations lose the productivity of those let go; those let go must scramble to find other employment; government funds are drained by unemployment compensation. The only winners are those clever enough, ruthless enough, or lucky enough to stay employed. Yet, if this practice is allowed to continue, those out of work will create an economic drain on the system and even the winners will become losers.

Forty Plus: A First Step

What do middle-aged managers or executives do when they find themselves unemployed? Well, it all depends. If they have prepared themselves, it comes as less of a traumatic experience. In the following paragraphs, we'll see why.

There is some general action that can be taken by all dispossessed managers and executives. First of all, there are books to read, some of them quite good and some not really very good at all, and organizations to join. One of the better books is Richard Bolles' *What Color Is Your Parachute?** An updated and revised edition has appeared each year since 1972. What comes out of this book is the admonition: "Stay productive." That is also the message that comes out of an organization called Forty Plus, whose sole function is helping unemployed over-forty executives and managers help themselves to find positions. Forty Plus has been in existence since 1939 and has offices in several major cities.[†] There is a fee to join, monthly charges, and an obligation to work gratuitously two days a week on one of the committees that are necessary for Forty Plus to function. Staying productive, which the club forces its members to do, is important psychologically.

What Bolles' book recommends, Forty Plus enforces, as illustrated by the following story. I met Arnie and Carl when I joined the Forty Plus club. Arnie had been with the club for over a year, but still hadn't landed a position. He told me that he had joined for a couple of reasons. First, it made him get up, shower and shave, get dressed and "come to work," if only for two days a week. Second, it gave him a base of operations outside his home. Although he was not as productive as he had been when employed, he was at least forty percent productive, working at the club two days out of five. He had also handled a couple of short-term consulting and development tasks on the side. He was surviving. About four months later, I learned that he had landed a position. By staying productive until he found steady employment, Arnie was in shape and up to speed when opportunity knocked.

Carl had worked for an organization that was not known as an easy place to retire from, so Carl, an accomplished information systems manager, had begun about fifteen years earlier to branch out and do other things. He did some teaching and set up a small business that he ran on the side. When he was fired, it was a sig-

---

*Richard N. Bolles, *What Color Is Your Parachute?* 8th ed. rev. (Berkeley: Ten Speed Press, 1990).
[†]For information about Forty Plus centers nationwide, call (212) 233-6086 or write to Forty Plus of New York, 15 Park Row, New York, NY 10038.

nificant inconvenience, but he felt that if he had not previously established these other interests, his job loss would have been a major disaster. He wasn't making much money, but he was staying productive. Despite all his accomplishments and his current activity, Carl confided that he felt insecure and anxious when he wasn't working, so he did his best to stay busy. Involvement in the club kept him in touch with other professionals and fueled his efforts in his own business. About a year later, Carl was grossing about $50,000 a year in his business and was teaching as an adjunct at two colleges.

COMMENTS

This chapter identified two groups of people that seem to share the same devotion to productivity: One group is made up of seasoned veterans of the business and industrial community; the other consists of people in their late teens or early twenties who are in college or are about to graduate from college and enter the workplace. It has been said that some young people just want older folks to get out of the way, but my experience shows that many others understand the value of experience and wish to benefit from it. True, some older folks don't want to stay on the fast track, but they don't want to retire, either. They just want to slow down a bit.

The article in *Time* magazine referenced earlier in the chapter predicted that the scarcity of young adults could result in a labor shortage in the 1990s. I say there is no reason for a labor shortage. If there are not enough qualified young people to go around, then folks in their forties and fifties who were the victims of downsizing in the 1980s can fill any shortfall. All that is required is that these older people be willing to accept less compensation for either less work or a different type of work than they performed before. Working for less sure beats doing nothing.

6

The Honest and the Modest

Let's be honest: If I had brains, looks, and a dynamic personality, I'd be unstoppable. Let's be modest: As things are, I feel like a combination of Rodney Dangerfield, Yuri Yosarrian, and Ensign Pulver.

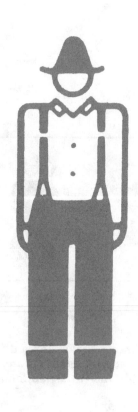

I guess that most of us would like to think well of ourselves. Yet, if we look closely, we all can see our limitations: We bungle things; we cause misunderstandings. Sometimes, despite our best efforts, we are ourselves misunderstood and as a result get treated unfairly. Why does Rodney Dangerfield get so many laughs with his "no respect" line? Because we all know how he feels. Some days, we feel threatened by the pressures of day-to-day life and for a while we, like Yosarrian, see the world around us as a giant insane asylum. There are other times when we are intimidated by others and we want to hide and blend into the woodwork like Ensign Pulver.

The business world is not one in which we should go around wearing our heart on our sleeve, but I don't think it's too much to ask that we admit about ourselves what everyone else already knows. A certain amount of candor and diffidence would not be out of place. There was a time, not too long ago, when the majority of people acted this way.

It constantly amazes me how we in the systems field allow certain people to lead us into endeavors that are not productive. I categorize those who mislead us into three types: egotists, pied pipers, and experts. The egotists know how to force others to give in to their desires. They are the easiest of the three to spot but the most difficult to deal with or eliminate. The pied pipers and the experts are seductive. Pied pipers lead us astray by promising easy solutions to our problems, while the experts overwhelm us with information and seem to have answers for all questions. I take a closer look at these three types of villains in the following sections.

EGOTISTS

My experience indicates that those who are boastful and arrogant are not more successful than those who assess themselves modestly. They just cause more trouble. In many cases, these individuals, through their aggressiveness, force their will on others and initiate projects and policies that are sometimes of questionable value. I have been at meetings where such people yell and scream and even throw things. Let it be understood that this kind of behavior can be effective.

87

Bullies

Very often, such bullies do get what they want. Sometimes, what they want is right and by forcing their will in certain situations, they may even increase productivity, at least for a while. However, these people often create an atmosphere of hostility and resentment; whatever productivity gains there might have been are soon lost as co-workers, subordinates, and even superiors work around them.

In situations in which the manager has the inflated ego, productivity can be severely impaired as subordinates become intimidated. I know of situations in which a group of competent analysts and their managers would go through great pains to produce an "everything is beautiful" report, just so as not to upset a superior with an oversized ego. Although they maintained a level of productivity, it was not as high as it could have been if they had not been required to "feed the beast."

Victims

Then, there are those who assess themselves modestly. Such people are sometimes taken advantage of by those with big egos, whether a peer or someone above or below them in the organization. When this happens, productivity is adversely affected. Generally, however, modest individuals do not cause as much trouble or resentment as those who are more assertive. Modest people generally increase productivity by allowing others to have and to express opinions. More often than not, two or more heads are better than one. When all of the individuals in a group are allowed to contribute what they know to a project, the result may well be a better product, a better service, or a better system, and a more productive team. I state this and stick by it, despite knowledge of the adage, "a camel is a horse designed by a committee."

We're not talking about a democracy here: There are leaders who do not require that everything be done their way. They encourage others to voice ideas and opinions, and then choose from them the best. Some diplomacy is required, since some of the ideas and opinions will be rejected either in part or in total. Yet, I know from experience that team members who have had a say in the way a product, service, or system is developed will be more productive than individuals on a team carrying out the orders of one egotist.

There is another reason why the individual views of team members must be considered and it has to do with group interaction. No matter which product is chosen, no matter which approach is taken, there are always going to be difficulties to be overcome. For the sake of productivity, groups first should perform a reasonable evaluation of alternatives; second, pick a software package, language, or technique; third, select an approach; and fourth, get going. Each team member must be involved during the evaluation process, so that all opinions and arguments are laid out on the table. At some point, the evaluation process has to end. At that point, have everyone involved either give their commitment to abide by the recommendations being offered or bail out.

Malcontents

Few things can hamper productivity more than one or two malcontents on a project who, at the first sign of difficulty with the chosen package, language, technique, or approach, say how much better it would have been if some other package, language, technique, or approach had been used. In order to maintain productivity, and to eliminate such disruptive behavior, the project leader must insist that all members of the team support the basic agreements made at the beginning of the project. If additional people become part of the team later on, it is imperative that they too accept the initial agreement. There may still be problems, but if team members have concurred at the start, then together they can overcome the problems.

PIED PIPERS

Although, at the outset of the 1990s, it seems that America has turned the corner and is again concentrating on productivity, we would do well to remember some of the sins of the last decade so that we do not repeat them. For example, we must not repeat the way many executives were made victims of the high-tech syndrome and the short-term cost-justification mentality.

Gurus

In the MIS area, for example, I have seen young self-styled gurus of information systems technology make some of the most impressive presentations, using the latest audio/visual tools, to razzle-dazzle even the most seasoned executives. To give them due credit, these pied pipers did do their homework: They knew all the specifications of the products or services they were proposing; they were aware of every generic organizational problem that the product or service addressed. What they lacked, however, was experience. Yet they still had the ability to intimidate and to create the impression that they knew what they were talking about. Occasionally, when seasoned veterans attempted to take issue with some of their proposals, they were criticized for being negative thinkers and were told that even raising such an issue revealed negative thinking. Rather than deal with the issue, the pied pipers put the veterans on the defensive. Although such action was an effective strategy in the game of one-upmanship, it rarely led to increased productivity.

Bad-Mouthers

Another example of how experienced workers in the 1980s fell victim to the high-tech syndrome was the pied pipers' bad-mouthing of existing systems. There are systems in every organization that could stand improvement, but by finding and highlighting the vulnerabilities of existing systems, the gurus created an impression that they knew what was going on and that they had all the right answers. The next generation of executives must be wary of people who seem to have all the answers and who are too sure of themselves.

I believe that those who are most sure of themselves in today's data processing environment are the most dangerous of all. Let's start paying attention to those who are *not* so sure of themselves, to those analysts and programmers who want to sit down with those who actually do the work to get their ideas on how things should be done. Let's listen to the programmers and analysts who have been employed by one organization for ten to twenty years to hear what they have to say about improving the environment. Let those who don't yet have the answers work with one another to see if they can come up with answers together. Perhaps then we'll see real progress and productivity.

Troops

Having been burned by the pied pipers of the past decades, present-day executives may view any new technology with skepticism. The troops in the trenches, who are for the most part unable to even approach the style and polish of the departed pied pipers, are unable to convince executives of the value of some truly worthwhile productivity tools. So they struggle along with technology that is obsolescent and the whole situation is restaged for the next group of pied pipers to come in, bad-mouth the existing conditions, and make a new set of grandiose prognostications about what they will be able to do with new technology.*

How about it? Have we learned? Can't we listen to the people we have working for us who have been with us for many years? Isn't it possible that they are loyal and dedicated and wish to improve the way we do business? We followed the pied pipers once, the young hot shots who told us how great everything would be, but we must be practical now and recognize that things may never be perfect. It is possible that at best they're just going to be tolerable. It is time to realize that, by following the young and the inexperienced and by ignoring or pushing aside those who are older and wiser, we are being ineffective, inefficient, and unproductive.

EXPERTS

To my mind, there is a distinction between the term professional and the term expert. I hold the professional in high regard. Experts I treat with skepticism.

Professionals

Let me define my terms. To me, professionals are craftsmen, individuals who know how to produce quality products or provide worthwhile services in a reasonable amount of time at a fair price. Experts, on the other hand, are individuals who either profess to know all there is to know about a particular subject or are touted as such by others. It is my impression that there are more of the

---

*For an excellent illustration of this, see *The Reckoning* by David Halberstam (New York: William Morrow, 1986), in which the people in manufacturing—wanting to make better automobiles—were constantly put down by the hot shots in finance.

latter than there are of the former. So hungry are we for quick and simple answers to complex questions that we "create" experts to provide them.

Politicos

When I was younger, I thought that it took too long for others to do jobs and that their work was often substandard. For example, I thought it ludicrous to pay three electricians for twelve hours to pull forty coaxial cables through the ceiling, when I thought I could do it with one other guy in two hours. I thought plumbers charged too much for seemingly simple repairs. Mechanics too seemed to always be ripping me off and doing sloppy work besides. On the job, I remember very clearly how, as a young programmer/analyst, I thought that most managers were unproductive and politically oriented. I said to myself that when I became a manager I would do things differently. I'd get my staff trained using the latest technology; I'd show the programmer/analysts on my staff how to write the best programs; I'd explain to my superiors how to maintain the quality and integrity of our systems. I'd have standards, and above all, I'd never be "political."

Estimators

As I got a little older and tried to do some of my own electrical, plumbing, and auto repair work, I learned a few things; I began to change my mind about what was simple and how fast things could get done. I became a little more tolerant of the other guy and his problems. After I attempted a major repair job, I learned firsthand that experienced craftsmen do know what they're talking about when they make estimates. As I grew older and became "trained," I learned to respect estimates made by professionals, but I continued to distrust the prognostications of experts.

COMMENTS

In order to defuse the undue influence exerted by the egotists, the pied pipers, and the experts, we merely have to examine ourselves. I offer myself as an example. With all my experience, I am very much aware, not of how much I know, but of how much I do not know.

When I do systems work, I seek consultation with those who have experience or who have worked in the area. When I write books, although it is sometimes painful, I defer to my editors. When I teach, I pay attention to what is written by the students on the evaluation forms. Because I do this, I believe I increase my productivity. Although I have suffered some setbacks, I try to remain faithful to these practices. Honesty and modesty are qualities that, when fostered in a work environment, will improve the way people work and communicate with each other.

PART THREE
Case Studies in Productivity

This part contains five case studies depicting the victory and defeat of many principles upheld by this book. From my involvement in these cases, I have learned that obstacles can be overcome, but not without risk. Those who attempt to improve productivity are not always welcomed. Some people have attitudes that mitigate against suggested improvements in productivity. There are those who are threatened by productivity improvements. There are those who, because it was not their idea, will either actively or passively resist new methods or technology. There are those who are simply out to take care of Number One, and they see their success, or in some cases their survival, in conflict with the initiative of others.

You should be prepared to see some of the most productive people in these case studies fail in their efforts or lose their jobs. My intention is twofold: to reveal the ways in which productive change can evolve in a corporate environment and to show how organizations impair themselves by impeding this change. I hope that these narratives will encourage those working in the information systems field to be aware of the rise and fall of new ideas that takes place around them.

7

Technology Gets a Bad Name

A young man was inexperienced in libation. Wanting to learn of it, he visited several local watering holes. At one he had rye and ginger, at another he had scotch and ginger, at still another he had bourbon and ginger. Not feeling too well, he switched to brandy and ginger and finally to wine and ginger. The next day, suffering from a nasty hangover, he concluded logically that the ginger ale, being the only thing that he had too much of, was responsible.

—Anonymous

Once upon a time, there was a Corporation. In this Corporation, there were four groups. Each of these groups consisted of several divisions, with each division in essentially the same type of business as each other division within the group. HRW, a division within a publishing group, was a company that had been acquired by the Corporation. As was the case in many such situations, the acquisition had been less than friendly, especially at the middle and lower levels of the organization. Even after several years, there was still a fair amount of ill will. Nowhere was this more noticeable than between HRW's MIS area and the Corporation's MIS organization.

BACKGROUND

About five years after the acquisition, the Corporate MIS organization proposed that it absorb HRW's data processing operations function. This MIS facility, called the Data Center, already supported the operational data processing functions of several other major divisions in the Corporation and was able to make a good case for absorbing HRW's as well, stating that it was simply a matter of economy of scale. On paper, the financial attractiveness of centralization is difficult to refute: The numbers invariably can be manipulated to indicate that centralized processing is less expensive than localized processing. However, the productivity issue is less clear. Whether it can be proven that centralization increases or diminishes productivity, productivity decreases notwithstanding.

Despite the anticipated financial benefits, people's resistance to consolidation is always strong, simply because they face a loss of control. Consolidation results in a reduction in the size of the divisional empire and a corresponding increase in the Corporate empire. The power struggle at the root of the animosity is an accepted (if not publicly talked about) fact of all corporate life. The decision to transfer HRW's data processing operation into the Corporate Data Center facility led to a power struggle in which the introduction of new technology was a central issue.

Though a decade has passed since the events in this case study took place, such struggles go on today. Other organizations repeat the same mistakes, not only with the database management systems technology product used in this case study, but with other products as well. Let's look at some universal lessons about hampering productivity that can be learned from what happened at HRW.

In the Division

In 1974, the publishing division completed a feasibility study and found that its order processing and accounts receivable applications were approaching the end of their usable life cycle and were in need of overhaul. HRW's MIS vice president, Glen Quinlan, proposed that database management systems technology be used. As justification for this, Quinlan cited benefits listed in the promotional literature—such as files with multiple indices and logical relationships among data elements in different files, and having enhanced programmer productivity. Quinlan needed approval from the Corporate MIS function, since such ventures into new technology would require a significant investment of money. Patently, the Corporate people, for having been one-upped by HRW's initiative and for not wishing to appear negative on new technology, went along.

On the Corporate Side

In the Corporate MIS offices, albeit a bit late, a committee of Corporate MIS consultants and systems software technicians was set up to evaluate the database management systems software products currently on the market. The systems software members of that committee were acknowledged "heavy hitters" who understood the workings of systems software. There were also three consultants on the committee, who had among them more than thirty years' experience holding positions in the divisions' MIS departments as well as in Corporate's MIS departments, including the data processing facility. The members of the committee reviewed product descriptions and specifications from the major DBMS software vendors, visited facilities where the various products had been installed, and interviewed managers and technicians who had already used the products.

After a few months, they collected all their findings, summarized them, and put out a report. The committee chose three products, concluding that those eliminated did not have the features necessary to support the major applications contemplated by the HRW division. The three remaining products were TOTAL, IDMS®, and IMS/VS. After what they believed to be a thorough evaluation, they selected IDMS.*

PREPARATION FOR IMPLEMENTATION

While the Corporate committee was occupied evaluating the data-base management systems products, the members of HRW's MIS department began developing the logical model[†] of the application's databases and systems and programming specifications. On HRW's MIS staff was Don North, who had a brand-new title in the organization: database administrator (DBA). The division was way ahead of Corporate.

In order to catch up, Corporate created a manager of database administration position and put Lois Singer, one of the committee's consultants, into that job. Corporate also created a manager of database systems position for Drew Wilson, another consultant on the committee. Unfortunately, the assignments were mixed due to a misunderstanding. Lois, with the superior systems software skills of the two, was offered the manager of database administration job, a position requiring application skills; Drew, whose strength was in applications, was assigned the position of manager of database systems, which emphasized technical skills. Though the new positions got Lois and Drew out of their dead-end consulting jobs, this mismatching inhibited productivity as time wore on, because they were always second-guessing each other's judgment.

The first task of the manager of database administration and the manager of database systems was the building of their respective staffs, to support the installation, maintenance, and use of the IMS/VS database management systems product. (That's right! The committee had selected IDMS, but it appears that somehow, someone in the IBM organization managed to convince the senior Corporate MIS executives that, despite the committee's findings, IMS/VS

---

*Though TOTAL had the highest number of installed sites at the time, the evaluation showed TOTAL to be inadequate for the tasks at hand. IDMS was chosen over IMS/VS because it was judged to be easier and less expensive to support and maintain.

[†]The logical model describes the relationships that exist between the data elements (fields or clusters of information) that make up an organization's information (data) base.

should be used. A committee of seven talented people had, in addition to their other responsibilities, made an investment of time and effort to produce a report that was totally moot. And since most of the people on the committee were now involved with the development of database support, they just let the whole thing ride.)

The Corporate Staff and Its Role

Within a year, a Corporate staff of systems software programmers and DBAs was in place. A few years later, there were about a dozen people, including managers, on the Corporate staff who were charged with the support and operation of the database management systems environment and the facilities of IMS/VS, the mainstay product of that environment. They were evenly split between the database systems support team and the database administration team. The systems support team members were to install, maintain, and enhance the IMS/VS environment and tend the auxiliary products, such as a data dictionary product, a prototype database generator, and various monitoring, support, and control programs. The database administrators were responsible for creating and maintaining the source database structures in the data dictionary and their compiled control blocks in IMS/VS itself.

The Division Staff and Its Role

In the HRW division, there was a database administration function with two members whose responsibility it was to design logical databases that suited the application, and about twenty programmer/analysts in the systems development department, who were involved in writing application programs that interfaced with IMS/VS database structures. Both the programmer/analysts and the database administrators worked closely with the individuals in the departments that would be the users of the systems when they were implemented.

WHAT WENT RIGHT

There were four things that were done well in the installation of the new IMS/VS, four things about which there were no differences or recriminations on either side, whether among the troops or between the division and Corporate managers and executives. These were the creation of a standards manual, the formation of project teams, the balanced use of meetings, and the involvement of an auditor from the beginning of the project.

Standardization

A standards manual was put together, not just for the publishing division application, but was made comprehensive enough so that any division in the Corporation could use it. It included file and program naming conventions that conformed to existing Corporate standards as much as possible. Forms and screen layouts were set up for the various types of data structures that had to be entered into the system. Responsibilities for each of the operating groups were defined. All in all, it was an excellent manual that was instrumental in making DBAs and programmer/analysts productive.

Staffing

The project teams were another contributing factor in maintaining productivity. On each team, there was a Corporate DBA, a divisional DBA, a member of the database systems support team, an applications project manager, a representative from the Corporate Data Center, and a Corporate auditor. Sometimes there were other individuals involved, but never fewer than these key players. While the publishing division's effort was under way, three other divisions opted to go with IMS/VS for applications development projects. A project team was created for each, modeled after HRW's.

Meetings were held to monitor progress and to control the difficulties that arose. In the early stages of the development process, the project team meetings were held weekly, and then every two or three weeks. As the implementation grew closer, meetings were again held frequently, more than once a week if necessary. No meeting was conducted without an agenda, and no meeting was conducted until everyone had a chance to read the minutes of the prior meeting. The moderator of the meeting was usually the Corporate DBA assigned to the project team. Most disagreements were handled at the meetings; only a few were allowed to escalate to higher levels of management, where senior managers seemed neither equipped nor disposed to deal with the specific debates held in project meetings.

The idea to use an auditor as part of the project team was a result of the tenor of the times. After the difficulties many organizations had in the late Seventies and early Eighties, commitments to new data processing technology, especially to database technology, were aptly known as "you bet your company" ventures. Corporate MIS Vice President Jim Walters had mandated that an auditor would be part of the project team. Partly because it was mandated and partly because it made sense, the auditor was an accepted, if not always welcome, member of the project team.

WHAT WENT WRONG

As HRW's database management systems project progressed, WBS, another publishing division, opted to use IMS/VS for its order service and accounts receivable functions. Instead of having two of the same DBMS applications, the executives of the publishing group decreed that WBS's order service and accounts receivable would be integrated with HRW's. The integrated system was eventually completed, but it came in two years late and cost much more than what was originally estimated. This was a deciding factor in the dismissal of a project manager and HRW's vice president. However, a year later, thanks to HRW's project teams, the standards manual and the integrated DBMS system was cited by a leading trade magazine as the best of its kind in the publishing industry.

Despite the praise from outside the Corporation, on the inside, senior managers, in both the group and Corporate, lost their faith in the value of such delayed, costly technology. As a result, both database technology and the IMS/VS software product would get a bad name in the organization. Let's have a look at why this happened.

Conflicting Interests

From the outset, most of the executives in the Corporate MIS function did not want to get involved with either database management systems technology or IMS/VS. Since they themselves had not initiated the thrust into this technology, they only reluctantly accepted it. Their approach was to give it as little support as they could get away with, so that, if something went wrong, they could not be blamed.

The Corporate MIS organization, by unspoken consensus, was committed to a CICS-based on-line environment* using standard access methods. The resistance to database technology and to IMS/VS was based on their pride in having been one of the first organizations to establish a viable CICS environment. Other factors contributed to the Corporate MIS organization's halfhearted support of IMS/VS. First, the current CICS environment kept the responsibility for backup and recovery of files with the division's MIS department. Converts to IMS/VS would put that responsibility in the Corporate Data Center's lap. Second, the Corporate MIS organization itself was about to introduce two major pieces of technology, IBM's new Virtual Storage Operating System (OS/MVS) and their new data communications product, Virtual Telecommunications Access Method (VTAM™). The support of three new major technology products at the same time had the potential to seriously hamper the support overall.

None of this was lost on Lois Singer and Drew Wilson. They were responsible for providing a high level of service with a technology and a product that had only the reluctant backing of their superiors.

Inadequate Estimates

The initial hardware estimates made for all this new software were woefully inadequate. It is a common mistake when, in attempting to determine storage requirements for a database management systems product, the estimate is about half of what it should be. This is simply because people forget that at least two copies of the software and the files are needed, one for production and one for testing and development. The second copy is needed so that testing is not done in a production environment. Yet, I have seen, more than once, that people forget this when ordering database software. It is difficult for MIS executives who are being paid to make good estimates to go back to their superiors and tell them that they underestimated and that they need more money.

---

*CICS® stands for Customer Information Control System, which is an IBM software product used to support on-line processing of transactions. Later on, it was enhanced to interface with the database management feature of IMS, but in 1974, such an interface was not possible.

A common mistake in remedying this is to succumb to the temptation of low-balling the estimate in order to get funding for a project. Theoretically, once a project has started, it is more difficult to pull the plug on it. If the senior managers are reluctant to oblige when more money is needed, the MIS executive may mention that they funded the project in the first place and if they cancel now, it would reflect poorly on them. This practice can only be effective in the short run. This sort of manipulation tends to have an eventual backlash; the senior managers don't forget. When requests for future funding are made, the MIS executives find that the senior managers require much more justification.

In this particular situation, the MIS executives blamed IMS/VS, calling it a "resource hog." The ploy worked. It lessened the Corporate senior managers' view of database technology as productivity improvement. It became, instead, a costly mistake. For about a year, HRW's systems development effort progressed, but when the need for the production system and its files arose, the capacity wasn't available. For about six months, the managers at the Data Center were forced to play the old "trying to get ten pounds of feathers into a five-pound bag" game. Drew and Lois knew that there was some chicanery going on, but were understandably reluctant to accuse their superiors.

Failed Teamwork and Cooperation

Although the idea of the project teams was a good one, and most of the systems, programming, and DBA members worked well together, the political situation sharply reduced their effectiveness. Because of all the new technology, Data Center had the most trouble. Once it was determined that the HRW project was going to be delayed, cooperation between Data Center operations staff and the systems software folks, which was not tremendous to start with, deteriorated even further. As individuals began to feel threatened, their behavior changed. The Corporate MIS, the Corporate Data Center software and operations functions, and the divisional MIS departments became overly concerned with forming offensive and defensive political positions. Even within those functions, smaller groups mimicked their behavior. Everyone involved, instead of pitching in to see what could be done to bail the project out and make everyone a winner, put all their productive efforts into making sure that they and their departments would not be a loser. That behavior was in effect for about two years until the project was finally completed. I believe that if people had had different attitudes, the project might have been six months to a year late, rather than two years.

Early in the 1980s, a clandestine meeting was held among some of the senior managers of the Corporation, the senior managers of HRW, and some outside consultants. The Corporation decided that it should not support both the CICS and the IMS/VS communications features, since both performed the same function. Some questionable techniques had been employed to manipulate resource billing numbers in order to make the IMS/VS communications feature look more expensive than CICS. Since the major thrust of applications development within the Corporation at that time was for on-line interactive systems, this signalled the kiss of death for IMS/VS.

The senior managers and the senior MIS executives had no idea that the database feature and the communications feature of IMS/VS were separate facilities and that the database feature could be used independently of the communications feature. To them, it was database technology in general and the IMS/VS product in particular that had caused the two-year delay in the publishing application. Having been a participant in all those efforts, it is my opinion that some solid technology and a software product, IMS/VS, which at the very least was adequate, got a bad rap.

COMMENTS

In any large undertaking, no matter how well planned, some mistakes are going to be made, some misunderstandings are going to occur, and people, more often than not, are not going to band together to pull somebody's or some group's chestnuts out of the fire. In addition to that, it has become an almost absolute certainty that the large projects are going to be late and are going to cost more than original estimates indicated. Forgive me if that appears to be negative thinking, but my experience over the past thirty-five years indicates that it is true.

My first recommendation is that undertakings be kept as small as possible. Large projects have a dismal record of cost overruns, late deliveries, and outright failure. To whatever extent possible, break large projects into small components.

My second recommendation regards estimates. There are some projects that are by their very nature large (D-Day, or the Apollo Project, for example). If a project is large, make as informed an estimate as possible and then double it. As I mentioned above, low-balling estimates is a devious and unproductive way to get funding. It can only be effective for the short run.

My third recommendation takes the form of an exhortation. We need to find a way to temper enlightened self-interest with the common good. Perhaps the wisdom of one of our founding fathers could help us here. Benjamin Franklin once said: "We must all hang together, or assuredly we shall all hang separately." Those who worked on the Constitution were as diverse a group of individuals as ever gathered together to achieve a common goal. We should strive for such success.

This last recommendation suggests that if we can find ways to work together we can be more productive for our organizations. It does not suggest that we will be more successful as individuals. Of all the people who were involved in that new technology endeavor, those who remained with the organization after the dust settled were the "street fighters," one or two of the managers, and a few of the better technicians. The entire Corporate DBA staff was gone within two years. Its members were slowly cut off from any meaningful projects and in that way were encouraged to resign, which they did, after the decision was made to discontinue development with IMS/VS. The database systems support staff was disbanded and its members scattered to other places in the organization.

There were more losers than winners in that episode. I believe that if there had been more cooperation and less self-interest, which took the form of the not-invented-here syndrome (sticking with CICS and cooking the performance statistics to make the IMS data communications feature appear a poorer performer than CICS), the new technology would have had the support needed for success.

Within ten years of all this, the Corporation was taken over by another organization, most of its divisions were sold off, and virtually all the members of its MIS organization, which had become top heavy and inefficient, were terminated. One of the primary criticisms of the organization made by the consultants who had participated in the transition was that the MIS function was inefficient because it had stayed with old information systems technology too long.

8

A Maverick Succeeds

In order to make improvements in MIS operations, initial increases in expenditures are needed to realize eventual savings in the long term.

I first met Alan Curtis a decade ago, during an annual MIS planning session, just after he had been hired as director of MIS for CBS Records, Canada. At the time, I was director of MIS Planning for the CBS Records Group in New York. I did not know it then, but over the next five years I would have the opportunity to watch Alan overcome a number of classic difficulties frequently encountered in the MIS field. He directed the installation of modifications and enhancements that not only improved the performance of the MIS function, but did so at a reduced cost.

BACKGROUND

Part of my job as director of MIS Planning was to assist the division MIS vice presidents in the preparation of their MIS plans. In addition, I also had the vaguely defined task of "helping out wherever possible."

The vice president of MIS for CBS Records International (CRI) was responsible for the activities of the MIS function in New York City. He was also responsible via dotted-line relationships for the MIS activities of owned or partially owned CBS Records organizations scattered throughout the world, including CBS Records, Canada.

As director of MIS for CBS Records, Canada, Alan was responsible for the MIS activity of that organization. Those activities consisted of a typical mix of manufacturing, finance, inventory, order entry, and marketing applications.

HANDS-OFF PRODUCTIVITY

In the early autumn of 1981, Chuck Klein, who at the time was vice president of MIS for CRI, shared with me some concern he had about what was going on in the MIS area in CBS Records, Canada. The way he put it to me was that Curtis was a maverick who wanted to do things his own way rather than go along with CRI MIS or Corporate MIS recommendations. He asked me to go to Toronto as his agent to see what I could do about the situation. I agreed to go but

111

was a bit uneasy about what my role was. I had been around long enough to know how the line "Hi, I'm from Corporate and I'm here to help you" was received by busy line managers.

I called Alan Curtis and told him that I'd like to visit and get a rundown on what he was planning to do. I told him what my job was, what the situation was, and that he could think of me as a Corporate spy. He laughed and suggested that I come up the following week.

The Situation in Canada

On the first day of my visit, Alan spent about an hour with me going over the current situation and his plan. There were two main problems. They were running out of capacity with their current equipment configuration (a Honeywell DPS L66), and the existing applications software that was currently in use was beginning to show its age. It was so heavily modified that it could no longer be considered stable. Changes had been made on top of changes; consequently, the programs in the system were unreliable in their performance and inefficient in their execution, causing frequent delays in processing that hampered the normal flow of business activity.

Alan introduced me to his two systems and programming managers, Wes and Susan. Wes had been with CBS Records, Canada for a number of years and was responsible for the inventory management and order entry applications, while Susan, who had been brought in by Alan, was responsible for the financial applications. Each of them explained the existing applications and also what they planned to do over the next couple of years to remedy the situation.

I also met briefly with the president of CRI and with the chief financial officer. My visit with the president was a pleasant surprise: Here was a senior executive of a major corporation who had acquired three IBM personal computers, one of which he was using himself. He seemed pleased to tell me how he had given the other two PCs to Curtis to place wherever he saw fit. Curtis had given them to the MIS financial applications development team. The team in turn had learned to use the PCs and had passed them on to financial analysts. My conversation with the president lasted about twenty minutes and during that conversation, while he did not come right out and say it, I got the impression that he too had confidence in Curtis. Later, when I met with the CFO, he indicated to me that he did not consider himself an expert on MIS matters but that he trusted Curtis' judgment as well.

My Recommendation

On the plane going back to New York, I drafted a memo to Chuck Klein, recommending that he let Curtis do what he wanted to do, however much he might deviate from the overall directions suggested by CRI and the Corporate MIS. When I got back to my office the next day, I stopped to visit with Chuck and I told him what would be in my memo. I gave him my reasons. In one day and a half I had come to the conclusion that both Curtis and his two subordinates understood their applications and their environment quite well. I felt that they had the total support of their management and added that any attempt by either CRI or Corporate to interfere with what they were planning would be counterproductive. Chuck accepted my recommendation but asked that I visit CBS Records, Canada again in nine months to make sure that they were sticking to their plan. I agreed. I called Alan Curtis back and told him what Chuck had said. He sounded relieved.

On my return trip, I accompanied Alan and one of his project managers to some of the meetings that they attended during the day. I simply observed the way these people operated. I was more convinced than ever that they were effective. They had nothing to hide and had complete confidence in what they were doing.

Six months after my second trip, I turned over to another individual my job as director of MIS Planning for the CBS Records Group. It was the summer of 1982, and I was about to move into a new position with CBS Records, U.S.A. I suggested to my successor that he handle the situation the same way I did, and went to Toronto with him, so that he could judge for himself. As far as I know, he accepted my suggestion. From that time on, I kept in touch with Alan Curtis by telephone, just to see how things were progressing. I remained convinced that Curtis and his staff were performing a thoroughly professional job and I wanted to see them succeed.

HOW THEY DID IT

When Curtis took over, CBS Records, Canada had a Honeywell L66 computer with supporting software. This configuration supported an on-line order entry application and batch applications including inventory reporting, sales reporting, manufacturing reporting, cost reporting, artist and copyright royalties, payroll, accounts receivable, accounts payable, publishing royalties, fixed assets reporting, and financial ledger. The programming language was COBOL 68.

Using a Service Bureau

Within a year of his arrival, in order to reduce the pressure on MIS Operations, Curtis moved a couple of applications and most of the development work to an IBM mainframe environment supported by a service bureau in suburban Toronto. Ten Harris 9200 screen/keyboard terminal devices and three Harris remote job entry configurations were leased on a short-term basis for the MIS analysts and programmers. I suspect that this would have been unheard of if CBS Corporate had been involved, and that CBS Records, Canada would have been required to use the facilities of CBS's Corporate Data Center.

During the same general time period, a new royalties system was acquired from CBS Records of the United Kingdom, was modified for use by CBS Records, Canada, and was installed and supported by the service bureau. The payroll system, which was being run internally, was turned over to a payroll service organization. A new chart of accounts was created and a batch general ledger package was purchased, which was also installed in the service bureau.

Investing in Equipment

About a year later, a used Ultimate D2 (Honeywell L6) computer and software configuration were acquired for internal on-line applications development. Following their acquisition, several new on-line systems were designed and coded, including a redesigned order entry system, inventory control, accounts receivable, and returns processing. In addition, an on-line accounts payable system was acquired and installed. All of these were installed on the Ultimate computer.

Returning In-House

It was in the following year that the savings began to accrue from the investments made in the first two years of the effort. Since much of the development and maintenance work could now be done in-house for the Ultimate computer, the Harris RJE configurations were reduced from three to one and the number of Harris terminals was reduced from ten to four. During that third year, the on-line systems that had been developed during the second year were installed. Since the major applications were now on the Ultimate computer, the service support for the Honeywell L66 was no longer required, so it was dropped. Because of the productivity improvements made in satellite activities on the IBM PCs, three more were acquired during that third year.

During the fourth year, an on-line manufacturing system utilizing bar-code and light-pen technology was installed on the Ultimate computer. The Honeywell L66 computer was bartered for a second Ultimate computer that was used for further development work, for administrative systems, and as a disaster backup.

By the fifth year, most of the major work had been accomplished. Costs and headcounts had been reduced. Enhancements and refinements were made to improve the overall performance of the installed applications. The second Ultimate computer was made fully compatible with the original for total redundancy. The PICK operating system, designed for on-line system support, was installed, and the on-line systems were converted to run under it, improving their performance. The outdated COBOL 68 batch systems were all converted to the more up-to-date COBOL 74 MVS environment at the service bureau. As the sixth year began, plans for the future included the creation of an on-line front end for the artist and copyright royalties system and the conversion to a fully in-house on-line system.

COMMENTS

Curtis and his staff were able to stick to their plan by applying MIS skill and plain business sense to the situation. There was an incremental increase in their headcount from 1982 to 1983 and a significant increase in MIS expenses. However, from 1983 to 1984, there was a small decrease in both headcount and MIS expenses, and then from 1984 to 1986, there was a dramatic decrease in MIS expenses matched by a continuing downtrend in headcount. The decisions to make these moves, made by Curtis and the management of CBS Records, Canada, undoubtedly would have been bogged down in a bureaucratic morass if corporate-level approval had been necessary.

Why did Alan Curtis and his staff succeed where so many others merely survive or even fail? There are several factors involved. First, Curtis performed well both as an MIS professional and as a businessman. He was not what some would call a technician, yet he understood totally what the technology could do and knew what technology should be applied where. He was resourceful in using the royalties system from CBS Records of the United Kingdom and in picking up the used Honeywell computer.

Second, Alan Curtis had confidence in his management skills and the support of his superiors. He understood the situation in both business and technical terms. He was able to direct the activities of his staff to apply technology efficiently to a business situation.

Third, Curtis realized that in order to convert to current technology from old technology, some doubling up of equipment and systems was necessary for a transition period. Those who try to escape this find that their costs are constantly increasing. Curtis proved that the increases in cost and headcount in 1982 and 1983 led to dramatic reductions in cost and headcount in later years. Without that initial investment, the reductions would never have been achieved.

A bit of irony: Alan Curtis left the CBS organization about halfway through the sixth year, because he was ready for a greater challenge and nobody could find anything better for him to do. Last I heard, Alan was doing fine; the loss was CBS's. Wes replaced Alan as director when Alan left and Susan left about a year later to start her own consulting firm. The end of this episode is not a tidy package, even though the accomplishments were significant. I'll leave the happy endings to Frank Capra.

9

An MIS Plan That Worked (for a While)

Any fool can plan; it takes a true executive to leap from crisis to crisis.

This case study describes the recovery process of CRU, a moderately large MIS function in a division of a prominent corporation. The CRU division, like HRW in the first case study, tried and failed to implement several major applications using the database management system product IMS/VS. So comprehensive had that failure been that it had made the senior executives of the organization realize the kind of impact that the MIS function could make.

BACKGROUND

There were three factions within the department. One was made up of the remaining veterans, those who had been there three years earlier when the ill-fated attempt at creating the marketing database system had started. A second group consisted of fairly recent arrivals who had been hired since the start of the marketing database system project but who were assigned to other new development projects. A third group was made up of those working on the marketing database system project itself. These had been relatively recent arrivals who had been hired to replace the vendor consultants involved with the project since its commencement.

The three groups were located in three different locations, and rarely spoke to one another. There was no coordination of their efforts and there was little love lost between them. The failure of the marketing database system had a devastating effect on the division: Quite a few people had either been fired or forced out, among them the vice president of finance, the vice president of MIS, two MIS directors, and several programmers and analysts. There had also been a number of voluntary resignations.

The Beginnings of Recovery

In the midst of this, Ed Baker was named vice president of finance and Mark McNair was promoted to vice president of MIS for the division. Both had been with the Corporation for more than ten years, but neither of them had worked for the CRU division before. Neither of them, however, had any illusions about the disorderly state of the department. In fact, one of the first decisions that they were asked to participate in was the cancellation of the marketing database system.

After that decision was made, meetings of all the senior managers in the division were scheduled. At those meetings, strategic directions were set for the MIS function, the most important of which were the reduction in MIS budgeted headcount, the moving of all MIS personnel into a single location, the development of a comprehensive MIS plan, and the creation of the Priority Book.

According to the plan, the Priority Book was to contain a prioritized list of all the projects that were to be undertaken by MIS. Projects were to be worked strictly on a priority basis; any deviations had to be approved by Ed Baker; no work was to be done on any project not listed in the Priority Book. A monthly meeting was to be held with the president and the senior vice presidents of the division to review progress on the projects and to see that there was agreement among all executives that designated projects were receiving proper attention.

A comprehensive MIS plan was to be the cornerstone of the strategic direction of all MIS activity that was to take place in the coming years. It was to include an executive summary, abstracts of business and MIS issues, explanations of overall MIS objectives, one-paragraph descriptions of all projects, and a complete set of financial and headcount budgets. There was a great deal of weeping and gnashing of teeth, but that plan was produced and it was a gem. It set the direction for the MIS department for the next five years.

THE 1981 PLAN

The Division Strategic MIS Plan for 1981 set objectives for the next five years and outlined in detail the first fifteen months. The Executive Summary stated that the MIS department would have as one of its strategic objectives the "enhancement of existing systems and the creation of major new systems." Specifically, one of the new systems was to be the creation of a data repository. Ed Baker saw this as a data structure that, without redundancy, would contain all the data elements used by the organization. Data would be entered into the structure only once, wherever the data elements hit the business first.

Another strategic objective was to get costs down to a level where they were a reasonable percentage of the division's revenue. Developing and stabilizing a skilled MIS staff, a constant refining of the MIS plan, and building enhancements to current applications were the other strategic objectives listed in bullet form in the Executive Summary. Although at times idealistic, the plan was taken seriously by those who prepared it, and that feeling spread through the division over the succeeding months.

Staffing Adjustments

During 1981, following the cancellation of the marketing database system, the three MIS staffs were consolidated into a single location. Dramatic improvements in productivity weren't immediately apparent. The political infighting increased as directors and managers among the three factions attempted to one-up each other. It would have been a trying time for an outsider, but since Mark had been with the organization for a long time, he had a good relationship with the veteran faction. He and the veterans knew the business and believed they could pull the three factions together, but recognized that it would take time.

The process proved difficult for the nonveteran managers and directors, and one by one, they began to resign. As they did, Mark promoted from within or went to other divisions to fill the vacancies with veterans. With each resignation and each promotion from within, Mark moved closer toward stabilizing the management-level staff. By the end of 1981, the staff was nearly stabilized.

Establishing Priorities

The Priority Book was a hassle initially. People had their pet projects and were reluctant to abandon them. Nobody liked filling out MIS project request forms and going around the people that they had always worked with, to get a director's approval. The applying of the ranking, which had to be explained and justified, was not much fun either. However, after a couple of months of doing it and finding that priorities did not change daily or even weekly, everyone involved began to appreciate the benefits of the priority system.

Upper management viewed the Priority Book effort as worthwhile, and saw to it that it was updated on a monthly basis and sent to the senior managers for their approvals. As vice president of finance, Ed Baker sat in on the monthly status meetings with the president and senior vice presidents of the division. What projects the MIS department was working on and how closely the MIS Strategic Plan was followed were under close review. Since Mark and his directors knew they had the support of the senior managers, they either curtailed, postponed, or canceled projects not in the Priority Book.

The Data Repository

The most significant item in the MIS Strategic Plan was the data repository project. This represented the division's commitment to the development of an integrated environment. But the division's senior managers were reluctant to fund the project. To them, it seemed too much like the fiasco of the marketing database system effort.

Ed Baker had to fight to get funding for the data repository. In 1982, he was able to open up a director's slot for this project and brought in Nick Calabrese from Corporate, a director with some database management experience. Nick proposed setting up an interactive mechanism for performing on-line maintenance on the division's major data elements and, in the process, eliminating redundant files. He also proposed that the four separately maintained customer files be merged and purged. The proposal was accepted. Nick produced an on-line mechanism, a security subsystem, and a centralized customer file. When implemented in the summer of 1984, this file was maintained centrally by four different operating functions within the division.

The Common Access Method

Another project in the Priority Book was to convert all applications to use a common communications access method, reducing the number of terminals required to support the division's applications. As a result, the number of terminals in use by the end of 1983 went from about 800 down to less than 600, a reduction of 25 percent. A year later, another 56 terminals were eliminated after the last three applications had their communications interfaces converted. Later, four new applications were added and other enhancements to existing systems were implemented without having to add terminal devices. This project stayed on track because it was part of the MIS Strategic Plan.

THE PLAN AFTER TWO YEARS

Toward the beginning of 1983, the division's president stopped attending the Priority Book project status meetings on a regular basis. Other, more pressing, matters were getting his attention. Taking their cue from their leader, the senior vice presidents started skipping the meetings also. Soon the meeting was held quarterly rather than monthly, with limited attendance. Accordingly, the process of updating the Priority Book was done on a quarterly basis as well. Pet projects began to slip back into the mix, many of them initiated by Ed Baker himself.

The Plan Unravels

In the autumn of 1984, after a decision to divide the CRU division into two separate components, there were no more updates to the MIS Strategic Plan. The MIS department had been split, with one director and his staff transferred to the manufacturing unit. Late in 1984, the division president resigned, not to be replaced until midway through 1985. The new president had no interest at all in MIS.

COMMENTS

Starting in the late 1960s and continuing through most of the 1970s, planning was considered to be the secret of successful MIS. As often happens when something becomes the "in" thing, it gets overdone. This is what happened with planning. Perhaps the 1981 planning document could have been produced with a lot less effort, but considering that planning seems to have been almost completely discredited and ignored, companies would do well to emulate the intentions of the original MIS plan.

In this chapter, I have described how an information systems staff was able to take significant steps to improve an MIS function for an organization. The staff followed a plan that had been initiated by the senior managers of the organization. It wasn't simply a matter of senior managers saying: "Do it!" It was a plan that made sense, from a business and from an MIS perspective. For about five years, the staff that worked in this environment was productive. The number of analysts and programmers that resigned in that five-year period could be counted on one hand. The majority of the members of that staff believed in the plan and did what they could to realize its objectives. To a great extent they succeeded.

From 1981 through the beginning of 1985, the MIS department had been extremely productive. The members of that staff had streamlined the processing, shortening the overnight batch processing cycle by about thirty percent, made significant reductions in redundant processes and files, and cut the number of terminals by more than thirty percent. They had simplified the operation of their systems by eliminating one of two communications access methods and one of two communications interfaces. The staff was stabilized; malcontents had resigned or had been laid off. The annual budget for the MIS department had gone from $13.7 million to $10.9 million between 1981 to 1985, a 23 percent reduction. All this was achieved as the actual workload increased. Too bad such success could not have continued.

To end all of this on a positive note, even though what is going on is less productive than during the five years covered in the 1981 MIS Strategic Plan, it is more productive than it would have been had that plan never been issued. It is somewhat more productive because most of the analysts and programmers who are still there were also there when the foundation was laid. Despite the lack of direction, they are continuing to add applications to the data repository whenever possible. The efficiencies made by eliminating the redundant communications access method and interface makes it possible to add systems without adding terminal devices. The elimination of redundant customer files and product files also facilitates the addition and the functioning of new systems. Earlier in the chapter, I called this MIS plan a gem. Indeed it was. The positive benefits are still flowing from its implementation.

10

An Executive Starts
His Own MIS

When a good product is developed, it doesn't have to be sold. It sells itself.

This case study describes events that occurred in the mid-1980s in a division of a prominent corporation when Ed Baker, the vice president of finance, sought an alternative to mainframe-based operations. He had read about the Metaphor® system in one of the business magazines, and was impressed by its potential.*

BACKGROUND

In brief, the Metaphor system consisted of a minicomputer acting as file server, equipped with a local area network to which PC-like workstations with graphic user interfaces were attached. The file server was able to hold summarized versions of mainframe files. Portions of those files could then be downloaded to the workstations.

Ed was a forward-thinking individual, and understood the value of a strong MIS function. He was an advocate of technology that enhances the imagination and productivity of its users. Much of the technology he had advocated up to this point had been mainframe-oriented, such as an MIS strategic plan and a data repository, but he had also experimented with PCs. Ed appreciated and understood the value of MIS technology in a strategic sense, but he did not want to be constrained by technological limitations. As chief financial officer of CRU, he had other more pressing matters to occupy his time. It also troubled him that, more often than not, information had to be rekeyed from mainframe-generated reports into PCs and then manipulated. He thought that unproductive and was bothered that he had to pay high salaried analysts to be data entry operators.

At the time, PCs had some real limitations, the two biggest being the amount of data that could be transmitted to them and the difficulties encountered in networking them. The amount of available storage was several million characters at best, and in many cases, single mainframe files were that big if not bigger. But Metaphor,

---

*This narrative is not intended as an endorsement of a particular product. Although I believe Metaphor is a good product and, when applied properly, can help an organization as it did with CRU, the purpose of the narrative is to illustrate how a forward-thinking executive can enhance a management information system in his organization.

127

with its graphic interface, minicomputer, and file server, caught Ed's attention.

The Metaphor System

The Metaphor hardware configuration consists of a minicomputer, disk and tape storage, a communications adapter, and networked intelligent workstations. The workstations are equipped with two megabytes of RAM, and come each equipped with a rechargeable, battery-powered mouse and both a manual and an on-the-screen electronic keyboard.

The Metaphor system software consists of an operating system, a relational database management system, a communications interface, and a standard set of utility programs. The workstations themselves have a mix of powerful PC software facilities, including a spreadsheet and an SQL* function. The user interface is an icon-driven multi-tasking facility. The software allows users of the system to create program-like icons of their own, containing programs or procedures. Analysts, for example, can create their own icons and save them so that the steps don't have to be recreated each time a function is to be performed. As of this writing, the Metaphor product has no competition, impressing even giant IBM, which entered into a sharing-of-technology arrangement with Metaphor in 1988.

Metaphor as a Marketing Tool

The Metaphor product was originally designed as a marketing tool, which could produce either summaries or subsets of historical sales information by extracting data from large mainframe files or databases and converting it into relational database form. The converted data could then be downloaded to a Metaphor system and made available to marketing analysts by means of their workstations.

The greatest value, however, lay in Metaphor's ability to make information available without the services of a programmer. The payback is that analysts could become more productive not only because they would have access to the same information as they did with terminal devices, but also because they could manipulate that information with the SQL and spreadsheet tools on their workstations.

---

*Structured Query Language, or SQL, is a retrieval language that enables users to create reports without having to write programs.

Programmers would also become more productive because they would not need to write or modify print programs, compile them, and run them in order to produce reports requested by the marketing analysts and executives.

IMPLEMENTING A MAJOR PRODUCTIVITY TOOL

Despite his awareness that the Metaphor system was targeted at the marketing function, Ed wondered if there were any reasons why Metaphor couldn't be used by financial analysts. Together with Bill Warren, CRU's vice president of MIS, Ed contacted the Metaphor organization and arranged to have the system demonstrated. Ed was impressed with the demo and began to talk with his superiors to determine if they could be sold on the idea. As originally specified by Ed and Bill, the cost of a basic Metaphor system with ten workstations was estimated at about $150,000.

Although there were many good reasons for the investment, Ed came up with two primary justifications. The first justification was time-related. Such a system would improve the speed of the month-end closing process, which currently involved the use and maintenance of a system written in an interactive programming language no longer supported by the company.

The second justification was staff-related, and assured that two programmers from the MIS department who spent virtually all their time writing programs to produce ad hoc reports for the finance and marketing departments would be freed up to do other things. This justification was intangible, that is, there was no way that it showed direct savings.

From the senior managers who were never sure when they would get their numbers, to the programmer/analysts who had to struggle through the process, everyone was dissatisfied with the current month-end closing process. Ed and Bill were convinced that Metaphor would improve the situation and they made a commitment to the senior managers. Ed transferred about $125,000, the cost of two programmers including benefits, to other more important information systems projects. Based on these commitments, senior management agreed to the purchase. Once Ed had been assured that the proposal for the Metaphor configuration would get all the required signatures, the negotiating process with the Metaphor organization commenced.

Getting Started

In the late spring of 1985, the Metaphor system arrived on the scene. Communications between the Metaphor configuration and the mainframe located at the Data Center a few miles away was an immediate problem. The communications feature was deemed too slow to transmit large volumes of data between sites, but the downloading of adjustments, which involve smaller quantities of information, was handled with dispatch. And so, once a summary version of the main database had been copied onto the file server, analysts could make adjustments to the main database on the mainframe and copies of those adjustments could be downloaded within minutes to modify the summarized database on the Metaphor system, resulting in operational improvements within CRU's finance department.

There were other minor problems along the way besides the data communications problem, such as periodic hardware and software glitches, fixes that didn't work, and breakdowns in communications between Metaphor technicians and the analysts and technicians in Ed's organization, but these were in most cases no worse than similar occurrences that take place in other areas where technology is involved. However, some of the analysts on Ed's staff seized every problem as an excuse to go back to the old way of doing things. All in all, as the months passed, the benefits of the Metaphor system began to outweigh the drawbacks. Except for a few diehards, most of the analysts came to realize that Metaphor was a significant factor in helping them improve their effectiveness and efficiency.

Day-to-Day Considerations

When the Metaphor system was first installed, Metaphor technicians helped the CRU organization set up the first database structures and also helped get the information loaded into them. Soon after though, they legitimately began to withdraw. But the amount of day-to-day commitment needed to support the system had been underestimated by Ed and Bill.

Within a few months of the Metaphor system's arrival, it became apparent that two functions had to be performed to make the system productive and to keep it productive. First, the MIS department had to provide a database administrator to design the relational database structures, to manage the allocations of space on the Metaphor disk packs, and to monitor and control the downloads that took place. Second, a system administrator from the financial analysis department was required to manage the library of programs that the analysts kept stored on the system disk.

The new database administrator and system administrator were sent to the West Coast to attend some classes that Metaphor ran to train people in those jobs. The enrollment fees, the plane fare, and the T&E expenses had not been figured into the original estimates. Not only that, but it didn't take long to figure out that backup personnel were required for both functions, for after all, people did take vacations, resign, get sick, and occasionally get otherwise preoccupied. Ed's need for additional financing was of concern but did not detract from the benefits the system brought.

Once Metaphor was in place, Ed really went to town. Whereas he had been awkward with keyboards and commands, he soon became a master with the mouse. He was pulling down information, manipulating it, and coming up with all kinds of observations and recommendations. He used the Metaphor system as a very effective management information tool. In addition, it was revealed to him that a feature could be added to the system that would allow him and others to use their workstations as 3270 dumb terminals also. The addition of the feature to the workstations made it possible to eliminate a dozen 3270s from the financial area. Of course, Ed opted for the feature and he soon had at his fingertips the kind of management information tool that he had always wanted and which he believed most executives ought to have.

Reaching Capacity

For a while, the system offered significant assistance: The month-end closing procedure was simplified and the two programmers were free to do other things. However, within three years, ninety percent of the disk space on the Metaphor system was allocated and about seventy percent of that was being used. Utilization was increasing at the rate of about five percent a month and projections indicated that even if some of the allocated space was released, the system would be out of capacity in about four months. Metaphor was popular; the financial analysts and even some of the folks in the accounting areas were asking for workstations. Five additional workstations had been added since it had first been installed, so that, in addition to the disk space problem, those using it were beginning to experience that bane of the mainframe user, response-time lag. It was obviously time to increase the capacity of the configuration.

The database administrator performed a thorough analysis and put together a document showing the current situation and the projections for the immediate future. He submitted it to Ed and Bill, together with two proposals and a recommendation. One proposal explained that for $210,000 the existing Metaphor configuration could be upgraded by doubling the existing disk capacity and by adding a feature to increase the speed of the processor. This alternative, although the less expensive of the two, would bring the existing Metaphor configuration to the peak of its capacity. The second proposal involved replacing the current Metaphor configuration completely with a new computer and two new disk drives, both reflecting new technology. The newer disk drives each had triple the capacity of the older ones and the new computer could support up to ten of the new drives. This left much more room for expansion, and it would be a long time before the capacity would be exceeded. The cost of this proposal was $355,000. Included in both proposals was a mandatory upgrade from one to two megabytes for all of the workstations because new releases of the software required it.

Because of the rapid increase in the use to which the Metaphor configuration had been put and the projections for future uses, the DBA recommended the second alternative even though it was the more expensive of the two. Ed accepted the recommendation and went to his management to request the new configuration. Evidently, Ed's superiors had been impressed with Ed's handling of the original configuration, because they approved his plans.

COMMENTS

As we have seen from this case study, except at the highest levels of senior management where it seems possible to make almost anything happen, individuals with ideas for productivity improvement must be prepared to go through a long, drawn-out process of selling their ideas to their management. They must go through channels and they must justify the expenditure financially or with believable intangibles. It took Ed a couple of months to find out whether he would get approval for the Metaphor configuration.

Once he determined that he would get it, there was a lot more paper-work before he could begin negotiations with the Metaphor organization. By persisting, Ed significantly increased his productivity as an executive by taking advantage of what information systems and computer technology have to offer.

The icon/mouse-driven workstation with its processing power, coupled with the distributed database capability of the Metaphor system, is a precursor of what is coming in information technology. The system's most important contribution to the CRU organization was the information it made available on a computer workstation that had previously only been available on paper. That information did not have to be rekeyed; both financial analysts and accountants could use it. As the analysts and accountants became familiar with the Metaphor system, their imaginations were sparked with new application ideas.

As an executive, Ed was on the leading edge, not just technically, but functionally. It's not that Ed had the most advanced tools available; it's that he did everything he could within a budget to make himself and his subordinates as productive as possible. That, of course, was his job, but Ed also proved himself to be a risk-taker. Unlike many others in similar positions who simply follow the crowd, Ed saw an opportunity and capitalized on it to the benefit of both himself and his organization.

11

Success Comes and Goes

Out of every fruition of success, no matter what, comes forth something to make a new effort necessary.

—*Walt Whitman*

The toughest thing about success is that you've got to keep on being a success.

—*Irving Berlin*

$\mathbf{B}$y 1986, it appeared that I had achieved success. All the trappings were there: the six-figure income, the four-bedroom house in the suburbs, two late-model cars in the garage, and four children who did not do drugs. I saw it differently. I thought of myself as a survivor, one who had managed to survive up to the present but who knew that my hold on all the trappings was tenuous.

My professional life has been a series of ups and downs. Some of my less-than-successful ventures have been the result of my own behavior, others have come about due to circumstances beyond my control. The same can be said for my successes. Yet, I continue to survive, and in the opinion of some, to succeed. In this chapter, I describe a series of events that show how a combination of good fortune and resourcefulness led to a success.

BACKGROUND

I started in the information systems field in the late 1950s and served my apprenticeship in operations and as a programmer/analyst. By the mid-1960s, I had become a manager, and, in 1970, a director. Although I held several director-level jobs after 1970, I realized that I had reached a plateau. In making the transition from programmer/analyst to manager and then to director, I became further and further removed from my hands-on skills and had to rely on managerial and political skills, at first to move ahead, but eventually just to survive. But politically, I was no match for most of the senior executives over me or for some of the managers below me. It was in the mid-1970s that I became more oriented toward survival than toward success. By the early 1980s I recognized a way to combine professional and personal interests.

A First Personal Computer

In the autumn of 1981, I tried to persuade my superiors to purchase one of the first IBM PCs. I knew that it would be an uphill struggle; word on the grapevine was that MIS executives looked upon personal computers as the pet rocks of the 1980s. Despite this, I persisted. I researched, composed, and submitted a complete configuration proposal but heard nothing from my boss. Knowing that my position was rather nebulous because my recent promotion had been arranged by senior executives rather than at the wish of my current superior, I thought it best to let the matter rest. Within a month, something happened to show me that I was no match for those with whom I worked: A new IBM PC arrived at the office of one of the young managers who was on the way up in the organization. The configuration was exactly the one that I had specified in the request I had sent to my boss.

Back to the Technology

Although I was annoyed by what had happened with the PC proposal, I put the incident behind me. However, a month or so later, I decided that there was another way that I could get back into some kind of technology again. I decided to go into the office early and work on BASIC programs before hours, during lunch, and after hours. I made friends with a few programmers who taught me the fundamentals of working with a mainframe workstation. Within a month, I was writing programs easily, and had acquired the skill of working interactively with computers.

Another Real Job

In the summer of 1982, I was named director of information systems of CRU, working for the vice president of MIS of that division. I was responsible for both database administration and the division's financial systems. Within a month of my appointment—and despite the fact that it was somewhat outside the scope of my responsibility—I prepared a proposal to acquire some IBM PCs. I believed that they could be used by individuals within the MIS department and the finance and accounting departments to improve their effectiveness and efficiency. The reaction of my boss was negative. Although discouraged, I did not give up. I decided to get a PC of my own.

In the spring of 1983, I bought an Osborne I portable personal computer. Complete with a word processor, a spreadsheet package, and standard and interactive BASIC compilers, it was the most inexpensive configuration around at the time. I improved my BASIC skills, taught myself some fundamentals, and discovered an effective and efficient way to learn how to use PC software. After preparing my departmental budget with the spreadsheet package, I showed a draft of the results to my boss, explaining the value of using formulas and the automatic correction processes. My boss simply pointed out the shortcomings of the draft, which was his way of telling me that he wasn't interested.

In the years that followed, I set up a small data processing operation in my basement while still holding the director's job. All that I learned about the technology I was using I shared with individuals in the information systems department and in other departments in the organization. But in doing this, I was digging my own grave. I was violating an unstated principle: I was refusing to allow myself to be completely controlled by my superiors and they did not like that. To them, my initiative was not as important as how well I could be controlled. I concluded this because I had seen other people survive simply because they allowed themselves to be controlled while creating the illusion that they were being productive. Nevertheless, I continued to develop myself through my outside interests.

THE RESTAURANT SURVEY

In 1983, I heard about a man, whom I'll call Gene, who was conducting surveys of restaurants among his friends. Each year he would send out questionnaires on which there were listed the names of about a hundred restaurants. Next to each name would be several boxes into which numerical ratings for food, decor, service, and cost could be entered. The questionnaires also had space for brief comments. When they were returned, Gene, his wife Anita, and some college students would tally all the ratings, compile the averages, and edit the comments. Gene and Anita had started this as a hobby but it had been such a hit with their friends that it grew each year, not only in respondents but also in restaurants covered. By 1983, they decided that a computer was needed to produce the next year's survey.

At our first meeting, I told Gene that I could handle the job. Together with my son Jim, I entered data from about six hundred questionnaires, each one containing ratings and comments for about fifty restaurants. It took us four weeks of working early mornings and late nights to get it all done. Gene was pleased with the results. Jim and I figured we worked for about thirty cents an hour, but we learned a lot. We agreed that we could have both spent several hundred dollars on classes and not learned as much.

An IBM PC Is Acquired

Early the next year, Gene called and asked if I'd like to work on the 1985 book. I was candid and told him that I had taken a bath financially in 1983 and would have to raise my price substantially. Since he and Anita were now charging for their finished product, he accepted my bid. Because Jim had other commitments and was unable to participate, I hired some college students part-time to key in the data.

The volume of questionnaires more than doubled in 1984 and so did the number of restaurants covered by the survey. It was no longer possible to do the job with one computer. Although I liked the Osborne, it had limitations that the IBM PC did not have, so I bought an IBM. The purchase turned out to be a wise choice, since Osborne's organization went belly up later.

When I started the project, I used both the Osborne and the IBM PC for data entry even though I had no real idea how I would combine the summary data when the questionnaires were finished, since the two machines were incompatible. I figured that in the worst case, I'd have the summary data from the Osborne keyed into the IBM. However, midway through the job, I found that I could get a modem and communications software for the Osborne for a mere one hundred dollars. The equipment and software was selling cheap since Osborne had gone bankrupt. I thought that this would be a good chance for me to learn how to get computers to communicate. I also acquired a Hayes modem and software for the IBM PC. It took a few hours of trial and error, but I finally got the computers to communicate, enabling the transfer of summary information from the Osborne to the IBM PC.

When the work for the 1985 survey book was finished, I had learned quite a bit about PCs and communications, made a few dollars, and was even able to take my wife and all my part-timers into New York to have dinner at restaurant number 577 on that year's survey questionnaire: Tavern on the Green.

1-2-3, an XT-clone, and a BASIC Compiler

When it came time to do the 1986 restaurant survey, it was estimated that the number of questionnaires again would double and the number of restaurants would be over eight hundred. In addition, another type of survey was planned, one which was to gather ratings for specialty food stores, wine and flower shops, and confectioneries.

In that year, I started farming out the work on a subcontract basis to other individuals who had their own computers. I simply made copies of the programs that were needed to do the data entry work and installed them on the subcontractors' computers. When all the data had been keyed in and summarized, I went around to the subcontractors and picked up the diskettes that I had supplied.

Also during that year, I used Lotus 1-2-3® for the first time to sort the summarized database, calculate a couple of indexes, and produce several output reports for both surveys. I acquired a BASIC compiler that enabled me to create executable programs, which simplified the operation of the programs significantly.

More Cities, More Software, and More Hardware

In 1986, by the time work was to begin on the 1987 survey, the number of questionnaires had increased to the point where I had to give the work to ten subcontractors to do all the data entry. They worked on it from April to November of 1986. Gene had asked that additional information from the questionnaires be keyed in, providing names, addresses, and other demographic information. Not only was it necessary to produce reports with overall totals and ratings, now it was necessary to determine the percentage of respondents by sex and age groups. Surveys were conducted in six major cities including New York. The addition of demographics increased the size of the files so that they were beyond the capacity of Lotus 1-2-3. This predicament gave me the opportunity to learn how to use dBASE III Plus® in order to handle the larger files.

In 1987, as preparations were made to produce the 1988 survey, the restaurant volume stabilized. Both the number of restaurants and the volume of questionnaires for the New York survey were up just a bit from a year earlier. Five more cities were done, but they were no more detailed than those that had been done a year earlier. What increased activity was the introduction of a hotel survey. This required modification of the data entry programs to accommodate the input from the hotel survey questionnaires, which were somewhat different from the restaurant questionnaires. Again, all the work was done on time and according to specification.

The Big Client Goes South

In 1988, as the plans for the 1989 guidebook got under way, Gene decided to try another organization to see whether it could handle the surveys at a more competitive price. It was becoming apparent that his organization had outgrown my ragtag but resourceful organization. He chose a corporation that was much larger and had access to a mainframe computer and a vast repertoire of resources. I prepared the data for only four cities that year; the other organization took charge of New York, Los Angeles, and the District of Columbia. In 1989, all of the processing was turned over to the other organization and I was left with little but memories of past glories. But, I had no regrets. It had been fun. I had proved to myself that I could meet challenges and use my resourcefulness to succeed.

Then, in early 1990, Gene called and asked if I could prepare a set of composite reports for all the most recent data of the cities that had been done so far. I assured him that if the other organization sent over their 1989 data, I could do the job within a week. The data was sent, processed, listed, and personally delivered back to Gene within six days. After that, I was given six surveys for the 1991 book and was asked to develop a database to create the various indexes used in the published books. The way things look now, I'll keep getting about half a dozen surveys each year. I am also working with Gene's organization to create a computer-based database of all the restaurants.

COMMENTS

In evaluating the years from 1981 till 1988, I simply compare them to what would have happened if I had not taken the opportunities offered. The biggest of these was getting involved with the surveys. Another was the rather unusual set of circumstances that led me to teach myself the BASIC programming language. If I hadn't proceeded independently, I probably never would have gotten the Osborne or have had a chance to tackle the surveys.

Like many people, I muse from time to time about things that might have been, trying to learn from mistakes as well as from successes. I left my job as director of information systems in 1989 by mutual agreement. In a way, it was like an early retirement, except that it was a little earlier than I had anticipated. It occurs to me now that my extracurricular activities, which I made no attempt to hide, may have had something to do with expediting my retirement.

But I do not regret the amount of attention I gave to my own business—even at the cost of my corporate job. On my own, I learned and practiced productive work habits that increased my self-confidence, even as I lost my steady annual income.

What can others learn from my experience? First of all, I never took on a job with only the current situation in mind. I was always thinking of the next time. With the surveys, I constantly built enhancements that might cost me in the current situation but that would benefit me the next time around. I tried to make every job and task a learning experience. Second, I did not always come up with the most efficient method of handling a task, but I got each job done on time and with a profit. Third, I did not cut corners. I could have hidden mistakes or fudged numbers. I did not do that; I did the work over at my own expense. Elsewhere in this book, I've indicated that individual success and project success do not always go together. If nothing else, this case study shows that resourcefulness combined with opportunity can lead to both individual and project success.

PART FOUR
Wisdom and Work

Part Four consists of two chapters that offer some proven practices on how we can increase our productivity, and a third that describes an economical and workable planning technique. The principles contained in Chapters 12 and 13 are those that I have attempted to apply in my own career and that I have observed others applying. I am convinced that these principles are both effective and efficient catalysts for productivity in project management. However, effectiveness and efficiency are not the only ingredients to success or survival, and so, in addition to the exhortations to use the methods, I also point out that there can be offsetting factors that prevent individuals from getting proper recognition for their productivity. In other words, if your aim is to improve your productivity, apply them; if your aim is to get ahead in a corporate environment, I suspect they may not always help.

Chapter 14 describes a planning technique that can be applied with a minimum expenditure of time and money. It has been my experience that most people who work in jobs that are operational in nature do not get excited about planning, but I can attest to the fact that the technique outlined here does work. While in an operational job myself, I participated in a group that used this technique on three separate occasions over a four-year period to plan projects fifteen months ahead. It became obvious to all of us that our department was significantly more effective and efficient after using the technique than it had been. The planning strategy gave the members of the department a better idea of what everyone else was doing, and how the actions of one group were related to those of others. In addition, nearly all the participants in the process enjoyed doing it; it was actually fun.

12

Management Principles

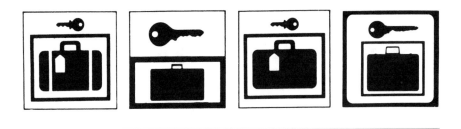

The longer we live, the more it seems that what we are taught about cooperation and teamwork is at odds with the way we must conduct ourselves in order to survive.

There are two aspects to successful management: success of the projects being managed and the success and survival of the individual managing the projects. At the first level of management (for example at the project-leader level), there is a much better correlation between project success and individual success than there is at higher levels. Barring the type of impersonal layoffs that come about as the result of some kind of consolidation or downsizing activity, one's skill, hard work, dedication, and effectiveness pay off at the first level of management and below.

At the second level of management and above, personalities become more important. Cynics, having been passed over, complain: "It's not what you know, it's whom you know." In actuality, it's a bit of both. The higher up in an organization individuals go, the more is expected in terms of effectiveness and dedication. At lower levels, they want your heart; at higher levels, they want your soul.

IMPROVING MANAGEMENT

My own views on productivity and individual survival have evolved over the years as I have learned more about how real work gets done in the corporate environment. The following principles continue to evolve and they have gone through several revisions since they were first published in 1972.* When I wrote the first version of these guidelines, it was approximately two years after a promotion to a second-line manager's position. A certain amount of skill, hard work, effectiveness, and dedication had resulted in my advancement. However, upon completion of a major project, I was surprised about who got credit, how much, and for what. I felt that I did not get proper recognition for what I had done. For the first time, I became aware of the fact that in addition to being productive, I had to spend time making the appropriate people aware of my productivity. This chap-

---

*For earlier versions, see "A Common Sense Approach to Management" in *Computer Decisions*, March 1972; "Common Sense Guidelines as an Aid to Project Management" in *Journal of Systems Management*, May 1978; and Appendix A in *Realizing the Potential of Computer-Based Information Systems* (New York: Macmillan Publishing Company, 1984).

ter and the next represent my current outlook of optimism tempered by realism.

There are times when significant increases in productivity are made possible through the introduction of some dramatically new methodology or through the accumulation of small improvements. This chapter is concerned with the latter. The caveat is that it is possible to be productive in terms of project management and yet to lose out in terms of personal recognition.

THE PRINCIPLES

There are fourteen management principles in this chapter. Each of the first eleven principles is paired with an opposing, Machiavellian viewpoint. The last three management principles incorporate counterpoints within their arguments. While I advocate what is described in the principles, the counterpoints portray a devious perspective that the reader should bear in mind. For every force, there is an equal and opposite force.

Write It Down

The technique is quite simple: Keep a piece of paper and a pencil handy at all times, and as tasks arise, write them down. As they get done, cross them off the list. This list can also be used for personal commitments. But don't overdo it; the list that I compiled while working on the 1970 CBS election system was about twenty pages long. The way I do it now, it is never more than a page. At one point, I began to think that the need for such notes was so obvious, that using them as a management guideline was superfluous. Then I noticed a number of what I would call successful managers using this technique. I don't mean to say that their success is due entirely to taking notes, but I believe it does help.

> *Machiavellian Counterpoint: Some would say, however, that the world is divided into two classes of people: those who do things and those who get other people to do things. Those who do things had better take notes and keep lists, since their livelihood depends on getting things done, correctly and on time. Those who get other people to get things done should keep lists*

of assigned tasks, but most don't. They simply get other people to get things done.

Match Your Knowledge to Your Job

When I first became a manager, I had more hands-on knowledge than those working for me. This lasted for about six months. At first the loss of that edge worried me, but I soon realized that to be an effective manager, I'd have to let my hands-on ability slide somewhat. I had to know enough to be able to manage a staff of competent technicians, but I also had to concentrate on the development of my management skills. This meant staying abreast of my field at the conceptual level. When problems came up, I had to delegate to members of my staff the responsibility to recommend solutions so that I could decide, after discussion, which solution to apply. I didn't need to know it all; I just needed to know enough to decide what to do.

> *Machiavellian Counterpoint: Although it's fine to adjust your skill to suit managerial responsibilities, remember that there are plenty of subordinates who hope to use their skills to advance themselves, just as you had. "Keeping your fingers" may be worth the trouble.*

Use Two Heads

The best way to play the management game is with others. Managers are often called upon to make proposals for new systems or improvements to existing systems. Before presenting a proposal, a manager would do well to get someone with sufficient knowledge (for example, a staff member, an associate, or a supervisor from the department involved) to try to find holes in it. Quite often, when proposals are prepared, some blind spots creep in, which are carried along throughout the analysis and design phase and are not discovered until the implementation starts. Although these blind spots are generally minor and only require a small amount of rework, they can cause considerable rework if they affect the logic of the system. It should be emphasized that reworking during the implementation stage of a project coincides with the period of time at which the pressure is heaviest, because of an approaching target date, and the coordinating of activities necessary to get the system into production. Earlier in the development cycle, these additional factors are not present.

> *Machiavellian Counterpoint: Using another person to take a look at a proposal in its infancy and plugging a hole or two at that early stage are productive and worthwhile to everyone involved. I have often done this, although sometimes I find it difficult when some nit-picking character finds a small fault in a presentation or proposal that has taken me hours to produce. Yet at the same time, I remember that this kind of criticism keeps me honest, and when all is said and done, I don't have to follow the advice if I don't want to.*
>
> *Bear in mind that while it's alright to ask the advice of others, be prepared to share the credit. There are those who are not above stealing ideas and taking credit for them.*

Keep It Simple

Esoteric language in speech and in memos and letters makes communications more difficult. The more ornate and flowery the language, the more obscure the message becomes. Instructions should be stated simply and precisely. If by necessity the instructions are lengthy, they should be written.

> *Machiavellian Counterpoint: There are times when communications are best when they are left vague. It results in a certain amount of flexibility later on.*

Keep Subordinates Productive

One of the best ways for a manager to keep subordinates productive is to create an environment in which analysts can analyze, developers can develop, and programmers can program. For a manager, this can mean taking responsibility for administrative tasks that tend to interrupt his or her staff's work. Specifically, managers should write the memos. Phone calls that are necessary for coordinating activities of a number of people should be made by the manager or a secretary, not by the analyst. If a group of programmers is working hard to meet a deadline, a manager can go for coffee, not one of the programmers. If a piece of hardware seems to be causing trouble, the manager should call the field engineers, not the programmer. If an analyst has a problem and wants to talk, a manager should find the time to listen. In my own experience, many hectic situations have been eased by the facilitation or cooperation of a manager.

> *Machiavellian Counterpoint: It must be pointed out that the somewhat idealistic scenario described above is based on the assumption that subordinates are motivated self-starters who require a minimum amount of direction to be productive. Among information systems technicians, especially programmers and analysts, my experience indicates that this is the case. However, the pressure on first- and second-level managers is increasing as their numbers are decreasing. Instead of finding ways to increase productivity, they are seeking ways to survive.*

Follow Up

Everyone needs some follow-up, if only to maintain proper perspective or interest in a project. If applied appropriately and thoroughly, follow-up can eliminate to a great extent the need to affix blame on someone who forgot to do something, or did something incorrectly. In the context of trying to get a job done as a member of a team, a follow-up inquiry is more effective than trying to be a star at the expense of others, or then saying, "I thought George was going to do that" when a project has slipped for some reason.

Follow-up generally becomes more important to a manager when he or she is dealing with people who are supporting a particular project or operation. The manager must understand that often these people have a number of other projects or operations to take care of, and do not have the same interest or involvement in the project as does the manager. Just as getting the manager's total job done consists of a number of things, so does theirs. Just as the manager occasionally forgets something, so might they. What they forget may be trivial to them; however, it could be quite important to the manager.

> *Machiavellian Counterpoint: The antithesis of follow-up is to slough off. The trick is to sidestep as much responsibility as possible by letting others assume more responsibility. This is an*

exciting process, especially when others are attempting to do the same thing.

Avoid Distractions

Some tasks should be undertaken as far removed from external distractions as is reasonably possible. Some managers find that working after hours provides an environment free from external distractions. But I would suggest that after a full day of work, a manager is more apt to be tired, tense, and upset. In the morning, however, there is a good chance that he or she is rested and refreshed. My own experience has shown that I am more motivated early in the morning than I am late in the evening. I have accomplished more by working for an hour and a half before regular hours than I would if I had worked three hours after a full day.

Machiavellian Counterpoint: Doing work early in the day rather than late has a couple of potential political disadvantages. First, nobody sees what time you come in, but everybody sees you leave. Second, there are those who work late and who look down on those who don't. If they are your superiors, no matter how effective you are, you'll have problems. Unfortunately, in a corporate environment, you may be judged more for appearances than for productivity.

Isolate Tasks

Every manager, at some time, has been faced with what appeared to be an insurmountable amount of work. When this occurs, stand back for a minute and take a look at what is before you. Break the pile of work into separate tasks. Practicing this idea does not reduce the amount of work, but it does put into clearer perspective the amount of work to be done. The magnitude of the work seems greater than it actually is until it is organized as separate tasks.

When confronted by a large number of tasks, separate them into groups and list them in order of importance. Then, tackle the ones you judge to be the most important first, regardless of size. In this way, there's a chance that some of those considered not so important might get cleared up along the way or turn out to be so unimportant that they need not be done at all.

Machiavellian Counterpoint: Many managers don't even need to bother themselves with isolating tasks into order of importance. They have found how predictably work will wither up and die from lack of attention. This is one of the subtle points that make management more of an art than a science.

Be Patient

Involved problems take time to solve. Many information systems managers were at one time programmers. Whenever they encountered a bug in a program, they sat down with the listing and found it. Some bugs were found in ten minutes. Other bugs took hours, days, or even weeks to find. Likewise, some management problems can be solved in ten minutes; others take longer. One of the differences between management problems and the problems of a program bug is that the management problems usually involve people instead of machines. When a computer "abends" a program, it kicks the programmer off, indicates that there's a bug, and gives the programmer a dump. It's clear-cut and there's no question about it. With people, it's not that clear-cut. People problems cannot always be solved with logic, fixes, or sets of rules.

My suggestion is to try patience; work with and listen to those who might appear to be rivals or opponents. Systems managers can meet resistance from department heads when they propose plans to solve a number of the company's problems. Systems managers should give their proposals time, discuss the parts affecting individual departments with the heads of those departments, and listen to what the department heads have to say. Above all, be patient.

Machiavellian Counterpoint: While being patient and practical can bring about good relationships, being forceful, aggressive, and unreasonable can get things accomplished that would not ordinarily get done—and faster. Those who practice forcefulness, aggressiveness, and unreasonableness are generally feared, grudgingly respected, and even occasionally well-liked.

Use Your Meetings Well

Meetings are often necessary, but by and large they are too long and waste time. The purpose of a meeting should be important enough to offset the loss of time to the attendees' jobs. To reduce the time an individual must spend at a meeting, try a modular meeting. For example, while two or three people must sit through an entire meeting, the three or four other people needing or contributing specific information can be called in and dismissed as necessity dictates.

The agenda and presentation of topics should be set up before the meeting so that the individuals who must be called in are summoned only once or twice. If they are called in more often than that, they will be ineffective outside the meeting and might as well sit in for its entirety. If information involving these people is discussed in their absence, the meeting's minutes should be published and all those attending any part of the meeting should get a copy.

A meeting should be set up if it has been found that dialogue between individuals is inadequate. A good indicator of inadequate dialogue between individuals is when small misunderstandings begin to take place. When people from departments within a group start to ask for everything in writing, a meeting is in order. Once a meeting has been set up, its purpose should be established ahead of time and an agenda should be published. Begin the meeting with agreement on the points that caused the misunderstanding, so that when the meeting has ended, those involved can go back to functioning as an effective group. A meeting should not be a witch hunt. Another solid reason for holding a meeting occurs when the departments working on a common project become so busy with their own work that they lose sight of what the others are doing. Periodic status meetings between department heads can keep the overall goal in perspective by giving each department head the opportunity to find out what the others are doing.

Machiavellian Counterpoint: Some meetings are convened so that certain types of people can show off how powerful they are. Try to avoid such meetings, but if pressed into one, speak only when spoken to, answer questions as succinctly as possible, don't volunteer information, and above all, don't try to resolve anything. Let the power seeker do what he wants and avoid eye contact with him. Some meetings are a net-spreading process. The pretext is to get enough people together to discuss a situation that appears to be in trouble. But the real purpose of these meetings is to catch enough people in a net of blame, so that the cause of the problems can be spread. Troubled managers should heed the advice: "When all else fails, convene a meeting."

Look After the Little Things

We've all heard the story about the million-dollar computer that couldn't run because the wrong $42 amphenol connector was installed. It's true—I was there. Twenty-four hours of processing was delayed, time was wasted up and down the line making phone calls to locate the proper connector, and a forty-mile drive from New York City to New Jersey and back was finally required to pick it up. For every project, many little things have to be done. For example: In order to get a terminal site working, in addition to the big things like electrical and air-conditioning requirements, one must assume the presence of little things, like the ribbons and paper. Don't laugh; I've seen a remote printer site all set up and ready to go with no paper.

The point I am trying to make here is a simple one. A manager should assign a specific individual to pay careful attention to small details before a job is actually started. Such careful attention early in a job will sometimes save the job completely. At the very least, it will reduce the amount of aggravation and confusion during the performance of the job.

Machiavellian Counterpoint: The heroes of projects are those who are responsible for the entire project, that is, the big picture, not the details. Taking care of little things is important, but generally not vital. The money, promotions, and recognition comes with total responsibility (including the little things). When taking charge of an entire project, make every attempt to find a low-key individual to take care of details who gets satisfaction from getting a job done and does not require the "big money" or the glory.

The management principles that follow have self-contained Machiavellian counterpoints, so there are none following them.

Accept Some Negative Thinking

There are some projects that just shouldn't be started; there are others that ought to be stopped. Positive thinking is often made such a priority that constructive criticism is thought to be destructive cynicism. Well-intentioned and experienced managers have raised legitimate objections to proposals or ideas only to be silenced by the retort that they were exhibiting negative thinking. While silencing may be justified in some cases, let us not forget that lifeboats on ships imply negative thinking, but they were precipitated by the loss of life on the *Titanic*. Seat belts also reflect negative thinking. So do error processing and backup and recovery procedures, which often represent more than half of the work that goes into an information system project. All of these necessities were prompted by negative thinking.

Always Have a Plan B

Having a backup or alternative plan insures a certain level of productivity—but not recognition—for the individual or group who advocates it. The practice makes so much sense that it is obvious, but it is often overlooked. When getting ready to cut over to a new system or when completing a major modification to an existing system, always have a Plan B. Although not much is lost if the secondary system is not needed, a great deal is lost if a needed alternative does not exist. However, do not expect to be rewarded or praised for setting up a Plan B, whether needed or not. It comes with the territory, something every responsible implementation team should include.

Try Small Project Teams

Small project teams are often more efficient and effective in achieving project goals than larger, more loosely structured teams. A small project team is a group of between three and six analysts and programmers brought together to work on a specific project for a set period of time. Since project phases are frequently different in size, scope, and duration, there is a good chance that the composition of the project team will change as a project is completed. However, attempts can be made to keep a nucleus of the team together for as long as circumstances permit. It is possible to promote within a project team or to move members among different teams within an organization.

In the process of forming small project teams, mix skills so that, by working together, the members of the team acquire one another's skills; for example, batch programmers learn how to write on-line programs and vice-versa. Members of small project teams also generally pick up a team spirit as they work together toward a common goal, giving credence to the old adage that the whole is greater than the sum of the parts.

The downside to small project teams is that it is difficult for the concept to work where there are traditional reporting structures. In order to be effective, small project teams (at least the nucleus) are like a task force, brought together for a specific assignment. When that assignment is completed, a new task force built around the nucleus is given another assignment, which may not be under the jurisdiction of the same manager. In an environment that is free from political infighting, the concept works well; where managers are jockeying for advancement, it doesn't work very well. In such an environment, managers constantly struggle to get the most qualified analysts and programmers on the project teams assigned to their projects.

COMMENTS

Project management and administrative management are very subjective. The higher up an individual goes in an organization, the more interested his superiors become in what he can get done for them and the less interested they are in how he does it. It may seem extreme to say that nobody above you cares about techniques, be they Theory X, Theory Y, participatory, or autocratic, but it is the truth in the vast majority of cases. Such managers are interested in results and in being undisturbed by situations that they're paying you to face. They are not interested in the specifics of their subordinates' careers because they are fully occupied taking care of their own. Once a person has achieved a middle-management position, future advancement depends on a combination of contacts, effectiveness, ability to communicate to specific individuals, and persuasiveness. Climbing the ladder requires a combination of skills, both productive and Machiavellian. As I stated in the opening, those who say: "It's not what you know, it's whom you know," are copping out. In the real world, it's both.

13

Communication Principles

What did you mean when you said that you thought that what I meant when I said that I thought that you and I both understood that what we had agreed upon was what he said in the first place?

The most insidious inhibitors of productivity are breakdowns in communication. Extremely difficult if not impossible to quantify, not readily discernible, and more damaging than appearances would initially indicate, these breakdowns are frequently the cause of much unproductive work in the form of memos, obstructionist tactics, and uncooperative attitudes. In this chapter, I propose some interpersonal communication principles that, if put into practice, should improve productivity.

The first constructive step that can be taken to deal with breakdowns in communication is to assume that they are going to occur more often than not. It is my belief that virtually every communication that takes place is faulty; that is, the communication is incomplete or partially misunderstood. The basic reason for this is that language is limited, even when both parties to a communication are speaking the same language.

IMPROVING COMMUNICATION

Let's start with the idea that each of us carries around a certain amount of cultural baggage as the result of upbringing, socialization, religious beliefs, and day-to-day experiences. Because of this, words, which are the basic building blocks of communication, have slightly different meanings to each of us. Some of us may even have incorrect ideas about some words; yet, right or wrong, that is what we think the word means. In addition to that, we also have mood swings and have preconceived notions about all sorts of concepts and issues. We each have our own ideas about what is worthwhile and what isn't, about what is the best way to go about doing something, and even about what constitutes productivity. We also have made evaluations about the other individuals with whom we communicate and they have done the same about us. All of this baggage has an impact on communication.

Now, this impact is not always negative. As a matter of fact, it can be helpful when individuals who have similar baggage are trying to communicate. Have you ever seen what happens when certain individuals get together, have a common goal, understand one another's part in achieving that goal, and then work together to realize it? It doesn't happen often, but when it does, it is a sight to behold.

THE PRINCIPLES

In the pages that follow, I suggest some commonsense principles that will reduce breakdowns in communication.* If applied universally, improvements in productivity will result. If applied unilaterally, there still will be improvements, but less dramatic. As in the last chapter, while I do not advocate the counterpoints, I list them in the interest of realism.

If You Don't Understand, Say So

Since most people in business speak in a jargon that is peculiar to their function, invariably something will be said at a meeting or during a conversation that one doesn't understand. Personally, if understanding a concept or a term determines how I am going to work on something, I ask for clarification. Judgment is required here. When dealing with an individual, in most cases it is a good idea to interrupt to get a clarification. At a meeting, I glance around to see how everyone else is doing. If they seem to be following, I hold my question temporarily, especially if there is someone at the meeting with whom I can later check. If the meeting goes on and I find that I'm getting totally lost because I didn't ask the question, I then interrupt and ask the question. If someone else interrupts and asks a question, I may try to tactfully tack mine onto it. If I judge that an explanation can wait till later, I don't interrupt, but make a note to get the information later.

When I deal with subordinates and I don't understand them, I interrupt and ask for clarification. If I feel that I'm having frequent problems in understanding a subordinate, then I call the person aside and discuss the situation, explaining that it is part of his or her job to communicate with me.

Machiavellian Counterpoint: I have been present at meetings at which senior managers and executives have been completely

---

*Some of the principles in this chapter represent their fourth published version since they first appeared in 1972. For reference to earlier treatments, please see the footnote at the beginning of Chapter 12.

intimidated by fast-talking MIS executives quoting facts and figures about nanoseconds, string switches, and other such computer configuration trivia. No senior manager or executive wants to appear less than totally knowledgeable in front of colleagues or subordinates, so no one questions the MIS double-talk. Experience has taught them that it doesn't pay to appear uninformed. Their personal survival is more important than overall productivity. There are times when we all must react to this Machiavellian truth.

Don't Waste Other People's Time

Some people won't let anyone interrupt them; their behavior may seem rude, but it is efficient. There are others who are polite and allow people to waste their time. In order to be productive, it is not only important that I not waste my own time, but also that I not waste anyone else's. There are a couple of ways of telling when I am wasting someone's time. The first is body language. Watch for telltale signs. A yawn is the most obvious. When the person to whom I am talking across a desk or a table leans forward, I believe that I've got his or her attention; when the person leans back, I believe he or she would rather be doing something else. Another indication of whether I've got someone's attention is the response I get. If the person asks questions or probes to get more information, I am communicating; if no questions are forthcoming, then I terminate the conversation or ask whether there is anything else to discuss.

Machiavellian Counterpoint: I have seen individuals waste the time both of the person they report to as well as of other people at a meeting. Not only do they get away with it, but they seem to enhance their standing in the process. It perplexes me. They seem to have the skill of making a little bit of responsibility and work seem like a lot. They do this by going into a great deal of detail about what they and the members of their staff are doing. They do this to impress the person to whom they are reporting.

Head Off Trouble Before It Starts

Quite often, it is possible to spot a potential problem before it starts. Managers of systems and programming functions are often familiar with many of the working functions within an organization and how they interface with one another. Occasionally, the people working in the departments are too preoccupied with day-to-day activities to be aware of a problem that is creeping up on them. When an outside manager notices a problem like this, he or she ought to tactfully inform those who are overlooking it and offer suggestions for some potential solutions. If a shift of current priorities is found to be in order, the decision should be acted upon; any delay will make a shift that much more difficult.

There are also other smaller problems that, if not corrected early, can lead to greater problems in the future. These come in many forms: for example, the project that begins to fall behind, the late report, the incorrectly entered input, and the like. Usually, problems can be resolved by some dialogue between the parties involved. Get the facts straight before the memos start. Every attempt should be made to try to get the parties involved to live with each other's occasional errors. Good feelings and trust between departments that have to work with one another are essential to a smoothly functioning productive organization. Many errors that take place are results of misunderstandings and lack of communication. The ability to successfully anticipate problems and help to solve them before they become serious, can enhance the esteem of any analyst, programmer, or manager.

> *Machiavellian Counterpoint: Although the above principle is useful in maintaining smooth operations, it assures the individual who practices it a complete lack of recognition. By heading off other people's problems, you may actually help inefficient or ineffective individuals to look good without ever forcing them to face the consequences of their mistakes.*

Attack the Problem

It takes mutual understanding and cooperation to define a problem and to resolve it. It also takes conversation. Hurt feelings and pride need to be put aside while the problem takes center stage. Quite often when one person or one group accuses another person or group of some kind of misbehavior or the violation of written or unwritten rules, the common response is defensiveness or counteraccusation. The "us-n-them" syndrome begins to take shape; opposing sides concentrate either on vanquishing the other side's position or vindicating their behavior. Productivity again becomes the loser as time and talent are wasted in a game of memo-writing and clandestine telephoning.

> *Machiavellian Counterpoint: No matter how much we'd like to sit down and work out problems and come up with solutions, nobody wants to come away from the situation labelled as the cause of the problem. Even in the best of situations, a certain amount of maneuvering will go on as individuals or groups try to come away clean.*

Weigh Your Name-Calling

Many times I have come out of meetings and, as the group breaks up and individuals get out of earshot, somebody is heard to say, "Boy, that guy Ralph is an idiot. He just doesn't understand the problem." For openers, there's probably a fair-to-middling chance that Ralph is saying the same thing about the name-caller. If allowed to continue, such mutual feelings of disdain are extremely counterproductive. People need to get together to discuss their differences and iron them out. Otherwise, all kinds of unproductive time will be spent compensating for the lack of communication between Ralph and his detractor.

Try to determine what makes someone seem like an idiot. For example, let's say Harry has been closely associated with a subject or a project for a year, and the purpose of the meeting is to explain to some legitimately interested people the reasons behind his methodology. As the explanation proceeds quite logically, based on what Harry knows from his close association with the subject or project, the listeners might become confused. Harry's very familiarity with the subject might lead him to omit some simple concepts from his explanations. One listener might interrupt with a question, causing Harry slight irritation. His answer to the question might reflect the irritation. The questioner might detect the irritation, become a little flustered, and not understand Harry's reply. The confusion then proceeds to compound upon itself. This is only one example of many reasons people come out of meetings thinking of one another as idiots.

Machiavellian Counterpoint: If he looks like an idiot, sounds like an idiot, and acts like an idiot, he must be an idiot. Sometimes, it is more advantageous to make the most of someone's apparent idiocy, particularly if one's superiors are inclined to agree.

Confirm Understanding—Repeat It

One way to overcome the problem of forgetting what we hear, is to repeat back what has been said *when* we hear it. In addition to helping us remember a communication, this exercise gives us a chance to confirm our understanding to the person who communicated it to us in the first place. Repeating something that has several parts to it has special value, since the more parts there are to a communication, the more likely we are to forget one or more of the parts. Repeating a communication enhances productivity because it's one way to avoid checking back later and it eliminates misunderstandings that would require time to resolve.

Machiavellian Counterpoint: Sometimes, it is more advisable to nod your head and forget what's been said. Repeating things has a way of obligating compliance to tasks that may not be to your advantage.

Close the Loop

This principle could be stated as: Communicate back to both superiors and subordinates. Managers and directors get together and reach an agreement—and then fail to pass the information down to the members of their staffs. In the information systems field, analysts and programmers and users get together, work out a resolution to a rather complex issue, and go off and start working on it, forgetting to tell their superiors or coworkers about it. Productivity is hampered in both situations.

Consider the following scenario: The managers and directors agree that the new chart of accounts that three analysts and a programmer are working on for month-end doesn't have to be done till three months later. Nobody tells the analysts and the programmer, because each assumed someone else would. Two days before month-end, the project leader tells his superior that the team has been working day and night to get the chart of accounts done, but he doesn't think they'll make it. Imagine how that superior feels upon hearing this! Imagine also the morale of the analysts and the programmer who have been putting in all that time! Clearly, their productivity will suffer for the next month or two. All this trouble because no one closed the loop.

> *Machiavellian Counterpoint: On the other hand, certain cases require more delicate handling. Withholding information that could save a subordinate time may be advisable—especially if it seems that he may soon overtake your position. Broken loops may help you get ahead, while others are left spinning!*

Listen

Listening is difficult. We live in a busy, fast-paced world that is full of distractions. So much of what is forced upon us in the form of advertising has made us resistant to listening. We are constantly bombarded with media messages. Yet, we have to filter out all the junk and pay attention to what's important. When communication takes place among subordinates and superiors, and the superiors are convinced that subordinates listen to and understand what the superiors are telling them, the superiors will trust them and let them get on with what they are doing. When subordinates believe that their superiors listen to them, they will be more productive and conscientious.

> *Machiavellian Counterpoint: Listening is a necessity of survival. You must not only hear what people say to you, but also what others say to others. This will reveal much of the unofficial power structure in a workplace. Listening is not as dangerous as repeating; you can hear your orders but still allow some details to pass through from ear to ear.*

COMMENTS

Some of these principles of communication are so obvious that it seems unbelievable that they would ever be violated. Yet experience shows me that they are violated. The Machiavellian counterpoints represent the most ruthless of these violations. When the communications principles are applied unilaterally, they will increase productivity. When someone puts into practice something that is worthwhile, other people are attracted to it and will follow suit. It is up to each of us to put these principles into action. By practicing them and discussing them, you can convince others of their validity and begin to improve productivity on a larger scale.

14

A Planning Tool

No one would ever think of allowing a multimillion-dollar airplane to take off without a flight plan and a destination, and then once up, of constantly telling the pilot to change direction. Yet we tell our information processing people to use multimillion-dollar computer systems to do just that.

This chapter describes a technique for planning the activities of a large corporate data processing center, covering a time period of about fifteen to eighteen months. The ideas herein had their origins at an IBM-sponsored planning session held in Palo Alto, California in February 1977. Activities were planned in monthly increments, and the technique was used in my organization three times in a four-year period.

The following characteristics of the technique make it attractive:

- The process is relatively simple.
- The setting is relaxed and informal.
- The facilities are minimal.
- The preparation takes less than a week.
- The participants get away from the office for two days.
- The materials and tools are relatively inexpensive.
- The technique is actually described as fun.

The use of this technique by the same group of individuals ought to be limited to about three times. That gives it a life cycle of about four to five years, assuming the generation of three fifteen-to-eighteen-month plans. Once individuals have participated two or three times in this planning process, their interest in it begins to diminish. It is then time either to change participants or to change the planning technique. Yet, for at least four to five years, the technique can be quite helpful in preparing an operational plan for establishing reasonable, reachable goals.

OVERVIEW OF THE PROCESS

The planning process consists of three steps: first, initial preparation; second, the process of laying out the detailed plan; and third, preparation of the Gantt Charts. The initial preparation process requires each participant to prepare a list of concerns and projects for the coming year. The process of laying out the detailed plan involves placement of milestone and task cards (described below) on a long, sectioned roll of paper called a calendar sheet. Finally, once all the tasks and milestones have been attached to the sheet, project planning sheets and Gantt Charts are made. As adjustments to the schedule are needed, the task and milestone cards can be moved. New Gantt Charts can be made up periodically to reflect the changes.

INITIAL PREPARATION

My organization chose October as a good time to hold the planning session. Projects were scheduled for November and December and for the succeeding thirteen to sixteen months. In order for the planning session to begin punctually and to stay on schedule, it is advisable for those living more than an hour or two away from the hotel or motel to arrive the night before. Some preliminary conversations and comparing of notes can be done over dinner. In that way, the participants will already be partially up to speed when the session commences on the following morning.

The Materials

The materials needed for this planning process are

- a rubber stamp, 1½ inches wide by 2 inches long, custom-made with six parallel, horizontal lines.
- a stamp pad.
- a roll of 20-pound paper, at least 36 inches wide and 30 feet long.
- a roll of ½-inch wide removable adhesive tape.
- a package of paper 8½ inches wide by 11 inches long, preprinted for project sheets and Gantt Charts.
- several packages of index cards, each a different color.
- one package of white index cards for each color used.
- black and colored-ink felt-tip pens, to match the colors of the index cards.
- two or three flip charts with easels.
- scissors.

Preparation of the task and milestone cards should be done prior to the meeting. Select about twenty cards from each package of colored index cards and five white cards for each colored card. Each card is then stamped with the custom-made rubber stamp, and cut down to the stamped size, ready for use as milestone and task cards.

The Planning Roles

The planning session for a large corporate data processing center will require the presence of those individuals whose titles match or are similar to those that follow: the director or general manager of the data processing center, the director of operations, the director of software support, the executive secretary, the manager of scheduling, the manager of computer operations, the manager of communications operations, the manager of operations technical support, the manager of database systems, the manager of personal computing systems, the manager of telecommunications systems, the manager of operating systems support, and the security officer.

In addition, one person is required to perform the function of moderator. This role can best be played by an external consultant, who is familiar with the functions of the group that is attending the session, but who has no specific interest other than in being instrumental in producing a workable plan. The secretary should assist the moderator in making the arrangements for rooms, meals, the suite in which the meetings are held, and whatever other accommodations are needed.

The Setting

While the use of the facilities of a hotel or motel increases the cost of the planning session, the expense can be justified in several ways. First, off-site meetings allow managers and directors to get away from day-to-day problems, giving them an opportunity to devote time to planning without interruptions. Second, managers and directors are given the opportunity to participate interactively with one another in putting together an integrated plan. Each participant is able to see how his or her activities depend upon or impact the activities of others. Adjustments to individual group plans, which probably would have been missed if plans had been made independently, are made in coordination with the department as a whole. Third, back on the home front, subordinates are given an opportunity to fill in for their superiors and to experience some of their problems. If subordinates cannot keep the data processing center running for two days, then the planning session should be postponed until they are able to.

A suite that is large enough to accommodate the entire group has some advantages over a conference room, primarily in that it provides a more relaxed setting. Informal continental breakfasts, coffee breaks, and cold-cut platter luncheons can be served in the suite. Lounge chairs, coffee tables, and sofas are less formal than the type of chairs and tables normally found in conference rooms.

The Schedule of Events

The moderator and the secretary assure that everything is in place so that the meeting starts promptly and moves along according to schedule. A typical schedule of events could be set up to look like the following:

Day 1

8:30 A.M.	Continental breakfast
9:00 A.M.	Statement of concerns
10:30 A.M.	Coffee
11:00 A.M.	Statement of projects
12:30 P.M.	Luncheon
1:45 P.M.	Review projects; assure that all concerns are covered by projects
3:00 P.M.	Afternoon break
3:30 P.M.	Form groups; prepare the detailed plan
5:00 P.M.	Break for evening

Day 2

8:30 A.M.	Continental breakfast
9:00 A.M.	Groups prepare milestone and task cards
10:30 A.M.	Coffee
11:00 A.M.	Begin laying out milestone and task cards on planning sheets
1:30 P.M.	Luncheon
1:45 P.M.	Continue layout of plan
3:00 P.M.	Afternoon break
3:30 P.M.	Make up project planning sheets
	Break when suitable

Since the atmosphere is an informal one, the moderator can begin bringing the session to order sometime in the morning between 8:45 and 9:00 A.M. For approximately two hours, all participants are encouraged to indicate their concerns about the coming fifteen to eighteen months. The moderator records and numbers each of the concerns expressed. There may be some discussion permitted as the concerns are stated, but it is not the objective at this point to address the concerns. A typical list of concerns recorded at a data processing center planning session might include the following:

- Increases in applications programmer productivity are adding to the processing load faster than the data center can acquire equipment to accommodate them.
- Systems software products are becoming so complex and are increasing in magnitude so quickly that maintaining reliability is difficult.
- Data security procedures need more attention.
- The job accounting system has been patched so often, it's ready to completely break down.
- Insufficient total resources are available for testing and development.
- Restart and recovery procedures for the on-line database systems are too complex operationally.
- Within six months, supplies of available telecommunications adapters on the front-end computer will have been exhausted.

During the first morning break, one can expect a lively discussion of the concerns and of how the projects can address the concerns. Often this is the first time that the participants have ever talked as a group about their concerns. Although there is always a certain amount of competitiveness in groups like this, there can also be a realization that, by putting aside differences, people can work together toward a common goal where everybody wins. In the meantime, all of the concerns that had been recorded and numbered on flip chart sheets can be taped to the walls of the suite. Typically, a group of around ten participants should develop a list of concerns numbering somewhere around sixty.

After the break, the moderator records and numbers the proposed projects put forth by the managers and directors of the various functions. The mechanics of recording and hanging the project sheets on the wall is the same as it had been for the concerns. Projects generally number between twenty-five and forty per functional unit, so that upon completion of this part of the process, there may be a total of more than two hundred projects. During this time, the secretary types drafts of the projects on standard sheets of letter-size paper. When the projects have been stated, discussed, recorded, and numbered, there is a break for lunch. During the luncheon, there tend to be animated discussions to assure that all the concerns expressed are covered by the proposed projects.

The early afternoon is spent correlating concerns and projects. The moderator again directs and controls the meeting. A cross-reference sheet is prepared in which the concern numbers are listed and next to them are recorded the projects that address the concerns. Discussions follow, during which unaddressed concerns are assigned to one or more of the three directors. Once the projects have been finalized, the secretary completes the typed list and makes copies of it for distribution to the managers and directors. At this point, the initial preparation for the plan is complete and, after an afternoon break, the detailed planning begins.

LAYING OUT THE DETAILED PLAN

It is the responsibility of the managers to rank their own projects according to priority. Each project is developed by a group of three or four participants. The directors move among the groups, advising and giving approvals to priorities. Priorities may change as it becomes more apparent how the projects of the groups impact one another; this may be the single most pressing reason for having a planning session involving all the groups.

Using copies of the project list prepared by the secretary, the managers and directors begin to identify the tasks necessary to complete the projects. Projects may consist of two to six tasks. The tasks represent the things that have to be done to complete the project. Elapsed time estimates are given to the tasks, and are used to estimate the duration of each project.

Milestones

Milestone cards are made up for each project and represent the completion of the projects. Each milestone is assigned the number given to the project on the flip chart. There is a card color assigned to the milestones of each project group. For instance, green might be used by Computer Operations, yellow by Scheduling, blue by Database Systems Support, red by Telecommunications Systems Support, and so on. A typical list of milestones in a data processing center's plan follows:

- Install the latest release of the operating system.
- Get the database management system operational as a production vehicle.
- Complete the conversion to the fixed-head disk drives.
- Complete the training for the interactive programming support function.
- Complete the conversion to the new communications access method for the manufacturing system.
- Configure and deliver the front-end computer.
- Complete site preparation for relocation of software programmers.

Tasks

The white task cards relate to specific milestones in two ways: They are given the corresponding milestone number and are written in the color ink that corresponds to the milestone card color. Tasks are also numbered serially within a project or milestone context. For instance, if milestone number nine had four tasks, those tasks would be numbered 9-1, 9-2, 9-3, and 9-4. The number assigned to milestones or tasks is placed at the upper right corner of the card. The task estimates are generally written at the upper left of the card. Descriptions of the milestone or the task are written in the body of the card.

The Calendar Sheet

After the milestone and task cards have been prepared, the next step is to lay out the plan onto the calendar sheet. This part of the process requires the most concentration, since it is the most detailed. First, the calendar sheet is hung on a wall. If the meeting is held in October, for example, the first month on the paper would be November, the second, December, and so on. We found we needed twenty-four to thirty inches per month for November through April, with eighteen inches sufficient for the remaining months. When using this technique, the details of projects are usually quite clear and precise for the first six months. As the plan projects further into the coming year, the details become less precise and more sketchy, requiring less space on the calendar sheet.

The task and milestone cards are placed on the calendar sheet. This process begins in the morning of the second day and continues into the afternoon. For a given project, a start date is chosen. The first task card is placed at that point. The next task for that project is placed in line horizontally, a distance equal to the estimate of the length of time required to complete the first task. This process is repeated for all task cards and finally the milestone card is placed in the same horizontal line at a distance equal to the estimate for completing the last task. All of the projects are handled the same way.

Schedule Adjustments

When all the cards have been placed on the calendar sheet, some schedule conflicts usually become apparent. For example, dependencies that had not been determined appear, such as the discovery that the manager of database systems had scheduled the installation of a new software product for June, but the product required a feature of an access method not scheduled to be installed until August. Or, the manager of operations technical support found that projects were scheduled so that during a three-week stretch in March there was work for five people but only three on his staff. The whole purpose of laying out the projects on the calendar sheet is to highlight what's going on, when it's going to occur, and where the conflicts are. The conflicts and discrepancies can be reconciled simply by changing the locations of some task and milestone cards.

Upon completion of the layout, approval of the plan is given by the directors. The remainder of the day is spent in the preparation of detailed planning sheets. These sheets provide backup for deriving the Gantt Charts, which are prepared to enable senior management to monitor the progress of the plan.

PREPARING GANTT CHARTS

Gantt Charts are used to provide a summary of the plan that is laid out on the calendar sheet. In all, there may be approximately two hundred projects, around one hundred and fifty of which are from, say, the software group and another fifty from operations. Each entry, or project, is backed up by a detailed planning sheet. As originally prepared, the Gantt Chart contains the name of the project and a thick solid line indicating initial and final dates for the project. When work begins on a project, a dotted line is used to indicate progress. If the start or completion dates change, a line can be used to indicate the new dates. An explanation can be provided for projects that are changed. Typically, Gantt Charts are updated on either a monthly or quarterly basis.

COMMENTS

Planning in a hectic operational environment is looked upon as an unachievable luxury. And yet the technique offered here does not interfere significantly with keeping the day-to-day operations going. For an investment of two days on the part of several people, the return is a clearer and more manageable set of tasks and projects. It also offers flexibility. I have seen the same organization operating both before and after using this technique. After being used, productivity increased. Common sense indicates that such planning activities would increase productivity; experience has demonstrated that they do.

Afterword

What was thought to be efficient and cost-effective in the short term has turned out in the long run to be neither. We did not pay the full price for our inexpensive products when we made them, so it seems that we have to pay the rest now. We produced products, primarily plastics, that were indestructible but not unbreakable. When they broke, becoming junk, we threw them out. However, they didn't rot; so now we're beginning to run out of places to put the plastic junk. We produced other products cheaply, cost-effectively, but we didn't take into consideration the cost of cleaning up wasteful by-products. Similarly, in the information systems field, quick-and-dirty systems, set up for the sake of expediency, are costing more now to maintain than they would have cost to properly build.

PRODUCTIVITY STARTS HERE

If there are to be improvements in productivity, they must be initiated from the top, in business and in government. In the recent past, the troops saw those at the top acting as if there were no tomorrow, so they assumed a similar attitude. When they saw senior managers and executives trying to get as much as they could, as quickly as they could, for as little as possible, they reacted in kind. Needless to say, this behavior did not increase productivity.

Although they are now encountering troubles of their own, during the 1970s and 1980s the Japanese put into practice the ideas and techniques that had made America productive (and wealthy) in the 1940s and 1950s.* In short, the Japanese taught the teacher. They increased their productivity by making quality products with less cost. We in America have now come to realize again, as we did in the Forties and Fifties, that in order to create real wealth and not just the illusion of it, we must concentrate more of our efforts on manufacturing and distribution than on finance and accounting.

In order to accomplish this, we must do several things. First, we need to avail ourselves of the capabilities of computers. We also need to reorient our thinking to effective and long-term as opposed to cost-efficient and short-term. We need to cooperate more with one another to produce quality goods and services. We need to approach each other with honesty and modesty and improve our communication. And we each need to make an effort to become more effective, resourceful, and productive, simply by trying to do our jobs a little bit better.

An Enlightened Use of High Tech

With a nominal amount of training, people can learn how to use personal computers to increase their productivity. A stand-alone (that is, not networked) PC is an extremely powerful tool. For anyone who works with columns and rows of numbers, a spreadsheet product can pay for itself in a matter of weeks or, at worst, months in increased productivity made possible by dramatic improvements in accuracy and speed. Writers can improve their productivity by using a word processor to make the creation of error-free documents a reality. Database management products enable nontechnical people to create and maintain large files of information, which they can rearrange and index, and from which they can selectively extract information and display either on a screen or on paper. All of this

---

*See David Halberstam's *The Reckoning* (New York: William Morrow, 1986, pp. 312-320) in which is described how W. Edwards Demming, frustrated by the United States' unwillingness to apply his proven principles to improve manufacturing, took them to the Japanese, who applied them with success.

can be done on a stand-alone PC without any help at all from a technician or a programmer.

Senior managers and executives also should avail themselves of the capabilities of computers. In the case studies, I have described executives who have been empowered by what they learned of computers. Using PCs connected to mainframes or minicomputers, they can develop procedures and programs to display the summary information that they need. In most organizations, the information needed to do this is made available on a daily basis. All that is needed to put together a system that will generate, at the beginning of each day, the most important information displays and a framework to produce others, are a results-oriented project leader, a programmer, and a few months of time. I have seen this done in a corporation with a very complex information systems environment. It should be done everywhere.

Long-Term Thinking

When it comes to investment (not speculation), we need to reorient our thinking to effective and long-term as opposed to cost-efficient and short-term. This is going to be a difficult adjustment because we have become accustomed to instant gratification. I have shown that short-term thinking and apparent cost-effectiveness in the recent past have backfired on us. Although we cannot possibly anticipate every problem, we can foresee some and those are the ones we have to address. We must listen to the negative thinkers. If an evaluation of the long-term cost indicates that manufacturing a product or providing a service is too high, then we should forego it until the cost can be brought down. In view of the current situation, it seems to me that we have no choice.

Greater Cooperation

Lily Tomlin once said, "We're all in this together—by ourselves."* This statement, both witty and pithy, can be taken as a warning, an amber light, so to speak. We need to cooperate more with one another to produce quality goods and services. Few of us are able to create functional goods and services by ourselves. We need one another.

---

*Fitzhenry, Robert I., ed. *Barnes & Noble Book of Quotations.* (New York: Barnes & Noble Books, 1987), p. 214.

Individual achievers are found primarily in the arts, and even most of them need help from others in getting their work the attention it warrants. As I advocated in the introduction, perhaps we should make the 1990s the WE decade.

Honesty and Modesty

We need to admit that we have limitations. We all make mistakes. I know that the majority of pencils I come across seem to have their erasers worn out before the shaft itself is even half used up. Because this is true, we must allow room for errors and leave sufficient margins in time and money to recover from them. In an environment in which making mistakes is punished, everyone is going to concentrate their efforts toward making it appear that they never make any mistakes.

I once observed a vice president of MIS who, when confronted with a problem that involved members of his staff as well as those of another department, said, "Okay, Charlie, we have a problem. I'll take half the blame, let's get it fixed, and get things back the way they should be. Then we can sit down, try to find out what went wrong, and set up a procedure so that it doesn't happen again." An attitude like this, if reciprocated, can eventually lead to a very productive environment.

Interpersonal Communication

It is my belief that not only do we lose opportunities to increase productivity, we actually squander them because of failures in interpersonal communication. In order to keep channels of communication open, follow the guidelines that appeared in Part Four:

- If you don't understand, say so.
- Confirm understanding; repeat it, or if necessary, write it down.
- Break complex tasks into as many discrete components as possible.
- Be skeptical of charismatic and otherwise impressive individuals (experts).
- Run ideas past another individual before going public.

- Attack the problem.
- Publish agendas, and use modular meetings.
- Listen.
- Close the loop: Pass information to superiors and subordinates.

These guidelines, will have a favorable impact on productivity simply because they lead to a more effective use of time. When interpersonal communication fails in a whole organization or just simply on a single project, time that could be used on some productive efforts such as writing and testing programs, is instead used in some unproductive activity such as getting back at somebody, or writing memos to justify and explain one's position.

RECONCILING WHAT OUGHT TO BE WITH WHAT IS

In my thirty years' experience in corporate America, I have found that what happens is not always rational. At times there is an *Alice's Adventures in Wonderland* and *Through the Looking Glass* quality to it all. In the corporate environment, there are Red Queens, Cheshire Cats, March Hares, Mad Hatters, Walruses and Carpenters, and even Tweedle Dums and Tweedle Dees. The first step that I take toward becoming guardedly optimistic is to acknowledge that, just as I look at people in corporations with a critical eye, there have to be those who look at me the same way. This helps me to understand that although I am, in terms of increasing or maintaining productivity, attempting to contribute to a solution, it is possible that I may also be part of the problem. Effective team-playing depends not only on judging others, but on identifying one's own weaknesses.

Besides the Tweedle Dees among us, some stand out in the corporate environment for their magnetism and productivity. Back in the 1970s, I met one man who really got my attention. He was Jim Geer, then chief financial officer of CBS. He said two things that made a lasting impression on me. First was a statement on his philosophy of reporting to executives or senior management: "If you can't say it on one page, I'm not going to read it." To that he added: "There could be and should be supporting documents, just in case I need them, but you'd better get your main idea or proposal in the cover letter."

Jim's single-page philosophy had been in place a decade earlier when he was instrumental in introducing the on-line system to CBS Television Network's sales force years before other networks had anything close to it. In those days, when virtually all computer systems spewed out large volumes of printed reports, Jim Geer wanted to use screens. He would often ask: "How many pages of the report can you read at one time?" Then he would answer his own question: "One. Well, if you had a terminal at your desk, where you could call up a screen of information, you wouldn't need all those damned reports." Due largely to the efforts of Jim Geer along with about ten analysts, programmers, and project leaders, CBS had an on-line system in the 1960s, nearly ten years ahead of all the other television networks.

The second thing that Jim Geer said that I paid attention to was his paraphrase of Reinhold Neibuhr's *The Serenity Prayer*:

> *Lord, give me the courage to change the things I can,*
> *the serenity to accept the things I can't,*
> *and the wisdom to tell the difference between the two.*

Interpreted in a corporate context, this prayer requests divine guidance in dealing with corporate politics. As I look back on my years at CBS, perhaps one of the most political organizations on the face of the earth, I can clearly see that from the ranks of middle management up, the survivors are few and far between. In fact, the current decade is proving that survival in corporate America is intensely difficult, political prowess or not. For a number of years, from the mid-1960s straight through the 1980s, there was an entrenched MIS organization at CBS that looked after its own. In that organization were some of the most capable political strategists that I have ever known. In the late 1980s, it all came to an end. There are only a handful of them left.

In the long haul, neither politics nor productivity guarantees continued employment. Yet if I have to choose, I personally will choose productivity every time, for three reasons. First, it gives me peace of mind; I know that given the chance, a reasonable amount of time, a reasonable budget, and a reasonable staff, I can always deliver a quality product. Second, through developing productive habits, I increase my resilience and self-reliance, which will help me no matter what the political climate is. Third, I was never very good at politics anyway.

In his inaugural address, John F. Kennedy said, "Let every nation know, whether it wishes us well or ill, that we shall pay any price, bear any burden, meet any hardship, support any friend, oppose any foe, in order to assure the survival and success of liberty." Noble words! But as high sounding as such rhetoric can be, it does indicate a direction: In order for America to increase its productivity, in order to survive, we as a nation and as individuals must be prepared to pay some price, bear some burden, meet some hardship, make some effort to support others, and prepare to encounter opposition. To quote again the young people from the *Time* piece: "We are the generation that is going to renovate America. We are going to be its carpenters and janitors.... We expect less, we want less, but we want less to be better."* As we approach the millennium, perhaps a new generation of workers will emerge, one in which the young and the old will join to rebuild a productive America.

---

*David M. Gross and Sophronia Scott, "Proceeding With Caution," *Time* (July 16, 1990), p. 57.

Bibliography

Bloom, Allan. *The Closing of the American Mind*. New York: Simon & Schuster, 1987.

Carroll, Lewis. *Alice's Adventures in Wonderland* and *Through the Looking Glass*. New York: Macmillan, 1923.

Dannen, Fredric. *Hit Men*. New York: Times Books, 1990.

DeMarco, Tom, and Timothy Lister. *Peopleware*. New York: Dorset House Publishing Co., 1987.

Drucker, Peter F. *The New Realities*. New York: Harper & Row, 1989.

Ellul, Jacques. *The Technological Society*, trans. John Wilkinson. New York: Vintage Books, 1964.

Fitzhenry, Robert I., ed. *Barnes & Noble Book of Quotations*. New York: Barnes & Noble Books, 1987.

Hackworth, David H., Colonel. *About Face*. New York: Simon & Schuster, 1989.

Halberstam, David. *The Best and the Brightest*. New York: Random House, 1972.

————————. *The Powers That Be*. New York: Alfred A. Knopf, 1979.

————————. *The Reckoning*. New York: William Morrow, 1986.

Krech, David, and Richard S. Crutchfield. *Elements of Psychology*. New York: Alfred A. Knopf, 1959.

191

Lasch, Christopher. *The Culture of Narcissism*. New York: Warner Books, 1979.

Lewis, Michael M. *Liar's Poker*. New York: W.W. Norton & Co., 1989.

Naisbitt, John. *Megatrends*. New York: Warner Books, 1982.

Pascal, Blaise. *Pensées*. Harmondsworth, Middlesex, England: Penguin Books, 1966.

Peters, Thomas J., and Robert H. Waterman, Jr. *In Search of Excellence*. New York: Harper & Row, 1982.

Pirsig, Robert. *Zen and the Art of Motorcycle Maintenance*. New York: Bantam Books, 1974.

Toffler, Alvin. *Future Shock*. New York: Random House, 1970.

——————. *The Third Wave*. New York: William Morrow, 1980.

Townsend, Robert. *Up the Organization*. New York: Fawcett Crest Books, 1970.

Wanniski, Jude. *The Way the World Works*. New York: Basic Books, 1978.

Wolfe, Thomas. *Bonfire of the Vanities*. New York: Farrar, Straus, 1987.

Index